TO DIE IS GAIN

Near-Death Experience and the Art of Dying Before We Die

JOHANN CHRISTOPH HAMPE

Translated by Margaret Kohl

Afterworlds Press

www.afterworldspress.com

To Die is Gain

PRAISE FOR *TO DIE IS GAIN*

"The accounts of the dying which he has surveyed and included in the text provide an empirical foundation, for all who are open to recognize it, for understanding the peacefulness and joy of dying."

~ Prof. George Fitchett, author of Assessing Spiritual Needs and Professional Spiritual & Pastoral Care.

"Hampe attempts to illustrate the experience of death as lived from within. He came to the conclusion that, far from being anticipated with fear and dread, death should be experienced as a gain. The presence of some commonalities in the accounts he collected made him conclude that these experiences were something more than dreams and hallucinations."

~ Prof. Ornella Corazza, author of *Near-Death Experiences: Exploring the Mind-Body Connection.*

"… an interesting book which examines, among other things, the testimony of some people who have clinically died and been brought back to life. … Hampe seems justified when he states that our present fearful attitudes to dying are not justified. It can be a release into a new and inspiring order of being. Most of his case histories are of people who expressed real regret at being 'brought back.'"

~ William Purcell, *Expository Times.*

"Hampe's unjustly neglected work represents the very first attempt from within the context of theology to investigate the phenomenon that only later became known as the 'near-death experience.' The book contains a number of virtues which might be expected to be of interest to anybody concerned to take such experiences seriously, especially theologians and philosophers. Hampe was the first to consider the implications of such experiences for our evaluation of mind-body dualism, the first to consider such experiences in detail in the light of Biblical teaching, the first to suggest that such experiences may be used therapeutically with the dying and the bereaved, and the first to posit the possibility that such experiences may have enormous implications for theologians more generally grappling with the problem of the meaning of death."

~ Mark Fox, PhD, author of *Religion, Spirituality, and Near-Death Experience.*

"Hampe challenges some of the traditional fears, presuppositions, and definitions concerning death and dying. The reader will find much of value in the first two chapters, in which the author draws together an excellent compend of reactions to death from a number of different disciplines and viewpoints."

~ *Concordia Theological Quarterly.*

"Well-constructed and lucid."

~ Prof. Ursula King, University of Bristol.

"Offers good practical steps for dealing more fairly with dying...No matter how we have lived in thought and deed, death is a beneficent leveler for everyone."

~ Prof. Ludwig R. Dewitz, Columbia Theological Seminary.

ABOUT THE AUTHOR

Johann Christoph Hampe (1913-1990) was a German Lutheran minister, journalist, radio broadcaster, and author of 25 books and many articles. He was born in Wroclaw, the son of a high judge. During World War II he was a soldier in Russia, then in Italy where he was captured by the Americans. During this time he was allowed to take care of the horses in a small circus, which facilitated his escape across the Alps on foot to Germany. His experiences of the war led him to study theology, alongside philosophy, and history in Göttingen, Tübingen and Geneva. Hampe traveled widely around the world, and was an ecumenical observer at the Vatican Council. To Die is Gain was his most famous and successful book, both in Germany and abroad.

No-one can have direct experience of what death is really like—unless it be the dying person himself.

(Otto Pieper)

This new 'I' was not the I that I knew, but rather a distilled essence of it, yet something vaguely familiar, something I had always known buried under a superstructure of personal fears, hopes, wants and needs. This 'I' was final, unchangeable, indivisible, indestructible pure spirit. While unique and individual as a fingerprint, 'I' was, at the same time, part of some infinite, harmonious and ordered whole. I had been there before.

(Page 75 of this book)

Man is so created
that his inner life cannot die.
For he can believe in God and can also love him.

(Emmanuel Swedenborg)

I simply put myself into this great hand of light ...

(Page 65 of this book)

A little space
and it is won,
the whole dispute
to nothing run;
in rooms of roses,
no joy unspoken,
with Jesus hold
converse unbroken.

(Kierkegaard's epitaph)

CONTENTS

TRANSLATOR'S NOTE

Every effort has been made to obtain the original texts of works in English cited by the author. In some cases this has not proved possible and a translation from the German has been given.

ACKNOWLEDGEMENTS

Thanks are due to the following for permission to quote from copyright sources:

Routledge & Kegan Paul Ltd and Princeton University Press: *Death and the Fool* from *Poems and Verse Plays* by Hugo von Hoffmansthal, edited by Michael Hamburger, Bollingen Series XXXIII, 2. Copyright © 1961 by Princeton University Press. Reprinted by permission.

Mrs Victor Solow and the *Reader's Digest*: 'I died at 10.52' in *Reader's Digest*, February 1975.

PREFACE

This book is the testimony of an encounter. I have been confronted
with the reports of people who were brought back to life although
they were actually dying, and who were able to tell us what they
experienced between life and death. I have put down many of these
accounts in the third of the following chapters, which comprises
almost half the book. The accounts surprised and bewildered me
and forced me to think afresh about what awaits us in the act of
dying. I was forced to surrender the notions I already had about
dying—which I had thought were incontestable—in order to
acquire new, clear, finer ones. The consequences for our dealings
with the dying and with our own deaths are incalculable; they are
already influencing my life today, although I am still in life's midst.
I have been happier since I have known the things told in this book;
and the response my lectures on the subject have met with shows
me how urgently the newly-awakened contemporary interest in
these great questions of life and death seeks expression and deepen-
ing. In the following pages we shall be entering a field where statistics and the multiplication table are useless and our usual ways of
acquiring knowledge take us nowhere. We shall never know everything, here. But why should we not, even in these ultimate ques-

tions, attempt to acquire the knowledge that is at our disposal? We could begin, as we usually do, with our prejudices and premises and the dogmas we have learned in the past, and then attempt to match these against experience. But the reverse method seems a better one. Knowledge can never replace faith; but tested experience will alter our judgements none the less. The person who is merely curious will not learn everything. The reader must co-operate in interpreting these phenomena. He is invited to take three steps—into yesterday, into today, and into tomorrow. We have seen dying from the outside: how have we related dying and death to ourselves up to now? After that we are permitted to look inside, to see what dying looks like from within—what it feels like. What does this new viewpoint tell us? We go on living with this know-ledge. What, thirdly, shall we—must we—do with it? If dying is after all quite different from what we have always thought, then our lives will be different too.

With all this we are still at the very beginning. While I was actually writing, I received new reports. I hope that this book will give many people courage to tell what they have experienced. But we have no wish to ring strange doorbells in the night, as spiritual-ism does. The reality of the soul is so unfathomable and so deep, and is so palpable to anyone with eyes and ears that we have no need to seek the darkness and the twilight in order to invoke the dead.

1. DYING BEFORE WE DIE

In the Midst of Life

It happens at some time or other to everyone who is wide-awake and aware. We are overwhelmed by it on a particularly fine spring day perhaps, and at the latest when we reach middle age. We always knew, but now it's gunpowder: there in front of us is the big black pit into which all life is ultimately going to disappear. It's not only all the other people—the people in the 'deaths' column. I am going to have to die myself. Who knows when? But because I don't know, death is already part of the present.

The idea spreads inside me. I can't think of anything else. The life that I pursued so painstakingly and so pleasurably—rain and sunshine, getting up and going to bed, all the successes and defeats which are my very own private affair—everything is going to be broken off. And one day what belongs together won't be allowed to be together any longer. Of every two people, one always has to be the first to set out: mothers leaving their children, a husband leaving his wife.

Some force takes us away. The moment flees. The hour never returns. People die on every side. But the time approaches, nearer and nearer, indifferently, moment by moment. The time will come when time will be without me. I find the idea an impossible one. Which of us ever stops for a moment to consider all the eyes that are just closing and the things that are sinking inexorably into the earth?

In this way the happiness we seek so passionately is related to death. For we call it happiness when the time that hunts us forward suddenly surrenders to us, seeming to stand still like a dragonfly that hovers, quivering, over a woodland pool. Then, for an infinitesimal second, uncounted by any clock, the thing present is suddenly everything; and for the space of a sigh we are whole and complete, a translucent sphere. We believed that in the light filtering through the birch trees and under the gold of the larches we could read the promise of permanence or, after all, of return. But it was always a deception.

Death is already present in my own life: this experience is the first point that I want to introduce into the reflections which we are preparing to share with one another. I am not talking about something in the distance, where everything is blurred, the end of life, which we think is a long way off. We do not want to satisfy our hunger for knowledge simply in order to have filled a few pigeon-holes in our brains with data—pigeon-holes into which we shall seldom or never look again. I am talking about dying because I want to live in a different way from before.

According to the popular view, when we die body and soul are separated. Popular opinion uses a simple vocabulary, not approved by the scientific psychology of our day; but after all there is some truth in its view. When I think about dying and experience it in the present, something in me is divided. I suddenly see myself as a stranger. Will what I am going to be, be no more than what I am now? What does the self in me have to say to this self?

Middle age is a crisis of being, just like dying. It is middle age that determines whether what remains is a withering or a ripening. At the peak of its vitality, in the years which are so often described today as the testing time for the person caught up in our merito-cracy, I either succeed or fail in uniting life's double span, to use the language of Johannes Tauler, the mystic.

Tauler distinguished between the pneumatic, or the mind-soul, life-span and the somatic, or body-soul, life-span. The one he con-ceived of in the image of a garland open at the top; the other as an arch open at the bottom. Both images of our present life, both arcs, he thought, touched each other at the tangent of middle age. Coming from above—or so the German mystic saw it—man is born into the physical world. But he is still called to return, and sets out on this return in the transformation experience that comes in the middle of life.

I see this book as a call to return of this kind. It aims to free us from the modern viewpoint, which I believe to be wrong. For we moderns always think that man's spiritual development is merely the reflection of his physical one. That is why we stare fascinated at dying as a biological phenomenon, if we think of death at all. That is why we need to prolong life at all costs, without enquiring whether the prolongation has any point.

For us moderns who belong to the western world, the mystic's two life-spans are opposed to one another. They have reversed their positions. The spiritual and the physical only touch twice, at birth and at death. In the decisive phase, middle age, they do not find a relation to one another at the tangent; they are at their furthest remove from one another. The person who is active in the world loses sight of his soul. Now the two arcs close and form a shell, a self-sufficient clam. Now the garland points downwards and the arch upwards, contrary to its true meaning. Man is no longer borne up from below and open towards what is above him; he is warped within himself. And he no longer knows that at a single point, the intersection of the tangents, the arches preserve the balance of the whole wonderful unity of human nature.

We see from this image that the unity of man is always in danger. Our right to dominate the material and our duty to serve the spirit strive in different directions. Dying is separation and separation is dying. The older we get, the more this fact will make us suffer.

Something tears apart within me. Separation does not only cut me off from another person. It separates me from myself. The body begins to break down here and there. Strength diminishes, illnesses crop up. Friends and relations die before me. The expectations I had had of them are disappointed. Successes which I meant to share with them dwindle away. The point of living is called in question. I

anticipate dying by experiencing what it is to be alone. I am alienated from myself.

More and more people round about me die, and death comes
nearer to me too. Will this one day be the ultimate act of dying,
when I experience utter loneliness? When his nearest and dearest has
been torn from him, the mourner feels as if he had died himself.
The muffled blow we feel when we hear the news of a death strips
us of ourselves, as it were. One day dying must be just as bad as
that. Was the beloved not my very soul? When body and soul are
one day torn apart in death I shall suffer the same torment.

But mustn't a person acquire more knowledge of himself, i.e.,
live his conscious life more profoundly, when he is thrown back
entirely on himself? The positive value of loneliness has often been
described. But it is only experienced by people who are free enough
to anticipate even dying as having a positive value. We shall be
considering whether this is possible. We shall be hearing accounts
which tell us that it is possible indeed.

The Fear of Dying and the Dread of Death
I am afraid because in imagination I can anticipate the future.
Through this fear I die in the very midst of life.

> The moment a person dies, the immediate impulse of primitive
> man is to leave him lying where he is and to flee. . . . The flight
> from the corpse is evidence that the man's fears are primarily for
> himself. To tarry in the presence of a dead person exposes the
> living man to the danger of being himself overtaken by death.[1]

Depth psychology says that the person who does not experience
horror in the face of death is inhuman and subhuman, like the boy
in the remarkable Grimms' fairytale who 'went out to learn how to
shudder'.

Up to the present day the sagas of the different peoples, with
their exhortations to accept dying and death philosophically, have
achieved little success against this feeling of dread. In their view it is
not death that is degrading, but our fear of death; for after all death

belongs to us in just the same way as birth. But how could anyone die willingly unless he despised life? The doctor looks on death as his enemy, because it compels his skill to capitulate. Every one of us who approaches his dying fellow and stays close to his side suffers under the general helplessness. And not many people will be able to cure their fear of dying simply by reaching for the Bible.

For the Bible itself talks too emphatically about the fear of death. Death cannot be viewed more radically than it is in the Old Testament, where it counts as the state where God abandons man. Death, we are told here, has its territory in the cosmos, which is not far off: on earth the depths of the grave, the sea and the desert. Life is surrounded by death on every side. We must not hope for heavenly dwellings in another world, but merely for the new era of salvation, when death will no longer rule on earth.

But we have to distinguish between dread, or awe, and fear. In our dread of death we shun and respect it. We preserve the distance that its majesty enjoins. Dread only turns to fear when we think of ourselves and try to save ourselves from the death that is inevitable. But dread is the tribute which we pay to death's tabu. Tabu, in the language of the New Zealand Maoris, means what is forbidden according to hallowed custom. The frontier of our existence is hallowed and tabu. Civilisation began with burial rites, and no-one evades this injunction down to the present day. The most enlightened free-thinker, who believes that man leaves nothing behind him after death and that he is simply a corpse, will follow a coffin with a solemn face. The most bitter enemies will see to it that their dead opponents are honourably treated.

We are not so much afraid of death as of dying. Since time immemorial the fear of dying has been based on three questions: when, how, and what comes afterwards? Who knows when it will be my turn? I cannot anticipate death, I can only make up my mind to it. And how easily I lose my equanimity simply by anticipating it! Some people, faced with the mystery of their lives, cannot wait for death and lay hands on themselves. But Artur Reiner has shown that suicide and wanting to die are two different things.[2]

The uncertainty which frightens me lies mainly in the fact that I cannot think of myself as having died. Today that counts as being an established fact of depth psychology. But Arthur Schopenhauer and Franz Rosenzweig (in his *Stern der Erlösung*) have already said the same thing.[3] To think of myself as having died means being able to command the moment of death. And it is the fact that this is not possible which makes the question so insistent and sudden death so mysterious and demonic. It disappoints the expectation of immortality which our subconscious keeps alive, even though reason and our experience of the deaths of our fellow men all round us confute it daily.

But today, it seems to me, it is the question 'How?' which frightens people more than the question 'When?' or the other uncertainty, 'What comes afterwards?'. *How* is death going to overtake me? is the question I ask about my own death. Since man as individual has an individual death, there are as many different ways of dying as there are people. How am I going to die? asks a person first of all, in his fear today. Quickly and painlessly, as he would like, or in pain, as he fears? Only few people are mature enough to accept pain and not to avoid suffering. But even the person who perhaps manages to do that in his lifetime will say that it is useless to go on burdening a life that is ending in any case with a long period of suffering.

We are frightened, for we shall undoubtedly be alone when we die. Fond of company as we are, used from our earliest childhood to get help from other people, we shall ultimately have to come to terms with this affair all by ourselves. No-one will or can take our place in this hour when life reaches its moment of crisis. The parable of the wealthy Everyman, whom none of his friends were prepared to help in his final hour of need, is valid for all time. Everyman is afraid.

In the end, Everyman in the story does not even beg to be spared death. He pleads for a single day, a single hour, he begs to die at the proper time. He is afraid that this single hour could be missing from his life; this single hour must not be allowed to slip after so many have been missed. The plea to die at the proper time is the expression of our desire for life to acquire a meaning, perhaps even at the very last moment. But is not just this the terrible thing about death, that it makes even the most successful human life meaningless, if it simply puts an end to that life?

Three things, therefore, make dying bitter for us: fear of the pain, fear of the ultimate loneliness, and fear of the futility. That is the way we see dying in anticipation. That is the way we experience it today, before we actually die at all. I accept the fact that I must die. It is the condition of my existence. But *how* I am going to die worries me. Am I right to be worried?

Is anyone prepared to say that nowadays the medicine chest copes with pain and that we ought to meet the futility of death by making our lives less futile? So that the only thing left is the loneliness? For death is simply the ultimate loneliness. Becoming utterly lonely, we die like a candle flame that has no more air. But even if this is all that is left for our fear to feed on, it is still more than we can endure: loneliness in the face of the power which is one day going to cut short our every word is terrible. We face the anguish that our life is going to be cut short in the pain of this loneliness, before we have done everything that we wanted to do, and had to do; before we have been reconciled with our enemies and have comforted our friends.

When will it be, how will it happen, what comes afterwards? The uncertainty, which we cannot disregard, becomes the source of our fear. Is the fear of dying unavoidable and human, just as, from time immemorial, horror in the face of the death tabu and the dead body has been considered part of human nature? The fear of dying that expresses itself openly, and the fear that consumes us secretly too, must be all the greater, firstly, the more we lose our sense of an order which extends beyond life and which imposes a duty on the living; secondly, the less we are able to have real knowledge about real dying, because we push the dying and the act of dying itself out of our world; and, thirdly, the more difficult we find it to expel from our subconscious the terrifying spectres which earlier periods, in their avidity for death, have passed down to us

Nightmare Spectres of Death
Our ideas about dying and death are neurotically loaded. The subconscious trails fears along with it which centuries have burdened

us with. Our contemporaries are detaching themselves without
much difficulty from the Christian interpretation of life, but they
cling grimly to medieval concepts of dying. Everyone still knows
that judgement awaits us and that it begins at the moment we die.
And judgement is a simple calculation, an unequivocal alternative,
the sheep on the right and the goats on the left, as Jesus told us.

There should have been good reason for Christians to love death,
since it after all opened up the way to the eternal kingdom of God,
the way which Christ took before us. But this early Christian
attitude was soon lost. From Augustine onwards, dying was understood as a punishment, physical death being the result of the Fall. It
was only nineteenth-century theologians, such as Schleiermacher
and Ritschl, who, after centuries of sermons preaching the horrors
of dying and death, dared to arrive at the idea that, for those who
are reconciled with God, dying no longer has the character of punishment but is a means of liberation from our earthly life.

The periods when death appeared in graphic visual form to
people have left their traces in our imaginations. In the thirty-two
plague years of the fourteenth century a quarter of the population of
Europe died, according to today's estimates. The plague returned
in every century, the bacillus that causes it only being discovered in
1894. Death came as the apocalyptic rider on his old nag, in
sulphur-yellow armour. As the Great Reaper with his scythe he
stood behind every door. His skeleton appeared on tombstones and
the frontispieces of prayerbooks. He swung his sickle over men and
women every day.

People saw their place as being under judgement. And it was the
judgement, not so much of a God of love as of the terrifying figure
of the bony, black man with the hollow eyes. The Redeemer who
understands the depths of man and recognises his aspirations
became the pitilessly avenging Lord before whom man flees to the
protective cloak of the Queen of Heaven and the arms of the saints,
with the intercessions they afford us.

The collective consciousness of this medieval heritage still has its
word to contribute when we contemporary people think of death
and dying. We are still tied to notions which our forefathers pic-
tured in their passion hymns. Death, still for Luther the evil enemy

of every night, became an ally of preachers who were supposed to be interpreting the Gospel of joy. Only the poor—who saw the evil social distinctions of the world annulled in death—were able to view it as friend and helper. The dances of death on the church walls, the calvaries and charnel houses along the churchyards, presented the picture of a death irreconcilable with life.

And when, at the beginning of modern times (which allegedly brought man's liberation), Johannes von Saaz for the first time made his 'ploughman from Bohemia' carry on the great debate with death, he too still remains caught up in the old spell. It is true that he is no longer prepared to accept death as the punishment for man's original sin and no longer recognises it as a law proclaimed by the same God who desires life. The writer even calls on creation to mobilise itself against the power of death. But the boundlessness of his grief over 'the cruel exterminator of all people', who took away his young wife on the feast of St Peter in Chains in 1400, also shows the fatalism of that period which, like ours today, was an era 'before sundown', to echo Hauptmann's phrase.

A hundred years later Paracelsus (who has been rediscovered in our own day) had still got no further in this respect. The mystical physician and 'brother Christian' proclaims the star of poverty and the kingdom of the supernatural, full of yearning pity for the lonely sick; in his four *Arcana* (the mysteries of the wise) he teaches values such as the overcoming of age, the renewal of the body, its purification, its rejuvenation, its lastingness—all of great importance to us today; yet he still pays death the dutiful tribute of the time. We are helplessly and powerlessly given over to this great enemy and destroyer. This is how Paracelsus lets death determine the division of the kingdoms: 'The good spirits receive the throne of heaven, and the evil ones the vale of hell, while to us God has given this earthly land as heritage.'

It is hard for us to rid ourselves of this mystical attitude to death. Neither the Renaissance, nor the Enlightenment, nor the liberal nineteenth century could get to the root of what forms the residuum of our foreknowledge here: death is the enemy *per se* and dying is consequently frightful, terrifying, painful, and threatening. As late as 1953 a professor of Protestant dogmatics addressed the following sentence to his 'unconverted' listeners over the Norwegian radio: 'You know that if you fell dead you would go straight to hell', thereby opening up a dispute which occupied his people for years.[4]

For generations the aim in life for many devout Christians was not to arrive at the hour of death in a state of deadly sin. But which doctor of the Church really knows properly what deadly sin consists of, and whether it is not, above all, a sin to talk about sin without at the same time talking about the forgiveness which Christ brought us—that was generally unknown to these devout men and women? And so it was hardly possible for them to do anything but to stray into death trembling. Jesus in Gethsemane is supposed to be an example of the fear of death. But he did not tremble at death, but at the greatness of the task which he was supposed to fulfil in dying. Fear, as we have described it and still feel it, is in contradiction to his fearless spirit. The devout heathen—Socrates, for example—have shown us that a man can die without fear under the most adverse circumstances. And we shall see what counter-forces are at hand in our souls to ward off all the nightmare images of dying and of death.

Powerlessly subjected to the hand of his murderers, his life totally frustrated, Dietrich Bonhoeffer achieved a death which testifies to freedom from hell's real terrors in our time. The doctor of Flossenbürg concentration camp gives the following account:

On the morning of that day between five and six o'clock the prisoners, among them Admiral Canaris, General Oster . . . and *Reichsgerichstrat* Sack were taken from their cells, and the verdicts of the court martial read out to them. Through the half-open door in one room of the huts I saw Pastor Bonhoeffer, before taking off his prison garb, kneeling on the floor praying fervently to his God. I was most deeply moved by the way this lovable man prayed, so devout and so certain that God heard his prayer. At the place of execution, he again said a short prayer and then climbed the steps to the gallows, brave and composed. His death ensued after a few seconds. In the almost fifty years that I worked as a doctor, I have hardly ever seen a man die so entirely submissive to the will of God.[5]

All Death Touches Us

Under the glass case of our prosperity we men and women see and do not see. The countless finely-adjusted mechanisms of the public welfare system preserve the tabu and keep death at arm's length. True, when the white ambulance screams past us because someone has caught it again, we jump nervously at our steering wheels. But as we accelerate again, our very next thought comforts us: they are bringing him quickly to the white hospital bed; the hospital people are sure to be able to help the poor devil. Every day we push aside whatever belongs to the tabu. No more people following coffins through the streets, no cries of pain in our ear, only seldom the miserable figure of the beggar, the cemeteries well out on the periphery. The death that affects me has emigrated from our everyday world. We have specialists to deal with it.

There is all the more for us to read in the papers and watch on the TV screen. There, every day, we face accidents and very often mass deaths and dying masses. We cannot close our eyes. We were never as well informed as we are today. But now comes the strange thing: the mass of information does not bring us nearer to our true human form. It actually hinders us from being people in true human form. We see with our own eyes the suffering that is going on over there, among the peoples with coloured skins; and yet we do not see it.

It would be too much. It would go beyond human measure. We cannot personally re-enact every death. If our mother and brother died, parts of ourselves, we would identify ourselves with them. But thousands in the China Sea? This is the way we talk. And we buy ourselves off with a subscription. The more there are, the less the individual catches the eye. The bitter deaths out there become for us an animal process, a saga that we listen to, the rumble of history; like genocide and the downfall of nations, it has its pages in the books. But of course we know that a person's death is never an animal process, whether it is a child's or a savage's (as we used to call the people over there), or whether it is on the slaughter-block, as the victim of napalm.

Modern sociologists would like to make us believe this. They maintain that the mass deaths which are possible today take away dying's individual character.[6] But the term 'mass', when it is related to people, only expresses a relationship. In certain contexts—in relation to other people and conditions, other methods of rule and other demands—man can be forced to give up his spiritual freedom; but he can never become in himself 'man in the mass'—not in every respect, at least, and probably never at all times in his existence. For otherwise he would have gone under as man. It is impossible ever to have total power over a person. Materialism cannot confute this belief. Even the vision of an over-populated earth, suffocating under its mass of humanity, remains a question put to men and women. If people do not survive, but merely the mass of dehumanised humanity, the whole thing loses its terrors in any case. For only people as people can experience it. Lao-Tse already recognised this: 'The reason why I suffer great misfortune is because I have a self. If I had no self, what misfortune could there then be?'

Every death of every person is therefore a personal death. It is only that we do not want to see what we know, or to recognise what we see. It is always only the first few seconds of the news. After that, complacency wins the upper hand again, complacency because it still does not affect us, because this particular death is 'over there' and still has a long way to go before it is 'in the midst of us', as it always already is, according to Rilke. So for us it all just remains death on the cinema screen, on TV, or in the papers. And the very quantity of news about death in other places has the effect of making us screen ourselves off, forcing death back into the tabu where primitive civilisations keep it.

But when we do this we are more primitive than them, to use the word in its false, negative connotation. The primordial man of primitive civilisations relates everything to himself, like the child. He has to fly from another person's death, because he already enters into it and pre-experiences it as his own. We consumers today grab at everything, but are more and more incapable of relating anything at all to ourselves. Eyes, hands, and stomach gorge, but the soul remains untouched.

Arnold Toynbee has told us that the middle-class family 'consumed' the deaths in South-East Asia, which were quite baldly presented to them on television as if they were something unreal; these people did not realise that dying was dying at all, because every evening, on the same screen, they were used to seeing actors playing out their deaths artistically and with practised skill.[7] In this milieu, death is a 'pretend', a 'finish' according to sporting rules, after which the objects of the show at once get up again and shake hands. The children of our generation probably see dying more often than children have ever done before, except for the children in the Thirty Years' War. But they actually see nothing at all, for what they are presented with is only the calculated 'killing' in the thriller which begins and ends with murder; whereas the sick grandfather, whose dying could tell them something, is quickly snatched away out of their sight and taken to the hospital for terminal cases. So the snapshots of mass deaths in the news magazine, like the game played by the murderer on the screen, which is enjoyably 'consumed' by the viewers, can even conceal the dying of the individual from us, because we become hardened. If we choose when to weep, we shall one day probably cease to weep at all; and a little later still we shall not even be able to weep.

Longing and the Death Instinct

But when I screen myself off, I am hiding myself. When I hide myself, I am afraid. This is what we are told. But the psychiatrists are unanimous in saying that people today are tormented much more by the fear of death than they were in earlier times. Our consciousness has many strata. Just below its surface, where we set up such cunning hiding places, the power of the death gods is at work.

It is the same thing with the tabu as with the Law in St Paul's writings: it attracts us and frightens us. We ought to keep it and want to do so, but we are forced to break it. Our generation is not free from this dichotomy, although it believes itself to be so totally enlightened. Both are present in our consciousness: at the top, repressed or freely admitted, fear of dying, fear of the pain, the loneliness, the meaningless which we suppose is part of dying; underneath, repressed or enjoyed with dionysiac fervour, the longing for death with its many modern forms, the breaking of tabus at every risk and at all costs.

We still praise youth as the only age worth living. We all want to remain eternally young and get our faces corrected and our wrinkles smoothed out so as not to let anyone notice that we have suffered for them. But suddenly death also enters into the present. The same young generation which is living at an age which we should like to see last for ever wears purple and black, the colours of mourning. Romanticism is rife: the form assumed by the soul's longing, nostalgia. Self-destructive forces arise: melancholy, black moods, depression, even despair make themselves felt in the very midst of a society of superfluity and surfeit which is still almost intact. The mind which at midday is aware of little except youth, life, and sensual pleasure drinks deep every evening of the black beauty of the Medusa, Satan's absurd metamorphoses, the half-baked wisdom of the Himalayan dream-dancer, the fatal symbolism of astrologers without a star, and the gothic tales of spiritualists without a spirit.

We have everything clenched, as it were, in our fists: knowledge of life's sweetness and death's inescapability, increasing information about the past and our incapacity to equal it, resignation over the sense of all our progress, with the continuance of the amenities it has brought us—in short the feeling of having everything and yet of not having a firm grip of anything at all, of being rich and yet poor, of avoiding death and wanting it at the same time, indeed, strictly speaking, of already being dead because dying is certain and because we do not want to recognise anything that goes beyond death. We shut our eyes to the dying of the multitude outside; but this contradicts our will to kill in masses, to discover new methods of torture and to expose our children to a sadism which, inquisitive about the sufferings of our fellow men, does not think about and count death but praises and eulogises it.

It is not remarkable that this disastrous, weary longing for death should have arisen. What are men and women really offered? What desires sustain their lives? Anyone who is alienated from Christianity because the Churches come out with their own words, rather than with the joyful language of Jesus, sees far and wide only pessimistic interpretations of life. Philosophically, the almighty science that dominates us has hardly got beyond Charles Darwin and Sigmund Freud. For Darwin death was merely the incision through which nature had to make room for new life. Freud, almost equally bleakly, described life as the tension between drives. Proceeding from the inorganic, life strives to return there. Not even progress and development are included in this viewpoint, only roundabout ways to death through the compensation of the drives; a process which admittedly becomes increasingly complicated the higher the organism is. What we should all really like to do, according to the theory of Freud's later years, is (through the compensation of our drive tensions) to sink back at once into the bosom of inorganic nature, into death, but unfortunately we have first to secure our way to death through the urge for power, the urge for recognition, the urge for survival. Everything that is lofty in men and women can be so interpreted, and must be so interpreted if life knows nothing beyond itself, and hence knows no depths to make its efforts worth while. What would love be, in this case? The most important 'principle of pleasure' which diminishes the drive tensions of which life consists.

So we arrive at this contradiction: our society represses death and deifies it simultaneously: we are afraid of dying and at the same time long for it as the ultimate escape. This is the way in which the person who is spellbound by death meets the tabu. And this attitude corresponds precisely to the secular idea of man that dominates us. In the tension between birth and death, the meaning of human life is to consist in the adaptation of the individual's drives to the collective drive of society. This is what Freud thought and this is what western society thinks, dominated as it still is by the spirit of a mechanistic science. Man is to adapt himself, thereby serving the collective economic and social goal of the classless society: this is what Marxism wants. Man is to adapt himself so that he can sacrifice himself for the glory of his nation: this is what Hitler wanted and this is the aim of fascism today and tomorrow.

In each case everything is shorn from man which goes beyond his utility and his attainments; and the rule of death is recognised in consequence. Death has to be deified in fear and awe if nothing is seen in man which points beyond his outward appearance to an 'eternal' destiny. Then death really is the almighty power. It constitutes man's boundary. Man is subjected to it. Bowed beneath this power, man experiences death before he dies.

Unless, indeed, he anaesthetises himself, screens himself off from this truth, flees. And then we have the vicious circle: where man is cut back to the utilisation of his span of existence, where he is unable to live the eternity that he really is, he has to repress death in order to go on existing at all. Repression becomes the expression of his fear. And this again prevents him from living his eternity and fullness.

Let us assume that this is how things stand with most people today. Let us not only assume it for the space of this introduction, but take it with us in the considerations we are about to share with one another. It is our firm intention not to turn our gaze away from the spectre. We do not know when we are going to die. That remains a cause for worry, for instance for the person who is leaving people behind him who are not provided for. But we can say something about *how* we are going to die, more than we knew up to now. And since our greatest fear is directed towards the 'how' of dying, dying itself could perhaps be transformed if we could give clarifying information at this point.

The child has first to learn how to shudder. Until he is nine, he hardly knows with any certainty that everyone, himself included, will die some day; from the age of twelve he takes over the euphemistic language of the grown ups; but right to the end of adolescence, dying and death remain embedded in the comforting pictures of tradition. But we cannot remain like little children, even if we ought to become like them. That is the difference: become like them, after we have known and because we believe. At the moment we have to endure the shuddering.

I said that men and women feel the breath of death's power at latest when they reach the crisis of middle age. At every swiftly running river, every time we hear of a death, we begin to experience our own deaths before we die. In dying—or so we fear—the bitterest pain awaits us; and the ultimate loneliness; and frustration in the loss of life's significance. Our idea of dying is neurotically loaded with primitive, nightmare images. That is why we flee from the sight of death and are yet simultaneously drawn to it. Most of us drive death away today and deify it tomorrow. We serve it and pay it homage. If there is nothing to be known beyond it, death, the great tabu, becomes the sum of our knowledge, the goal of our path, the ultimate destiny, irrefutable validity. It is almighty for most of the people of our time, and it is ever-present for us all:

O Death is great,
We smile
but we are his.
When we think we stand
in the midst of life
he dares to weep
in the midst of us.[8]

2. DYING SEEN FROM OUTSIDE

The Soul Goes Ahead of Us

I change in relation to the world. The world changes in relation to me. I communicate myself, I receive communication. That is what life is about: I and Thou change, participate in one another. Death ends our processes of alteration, forcing us to fall dumb. That is why death is not an event in life.

But dying still belongs to life. It is its final, critical stage. Dying is the part of life which goes out towards death. Since all life proceeds towards death, all life is in actual fact a dying; we have already made this clear to ourselves. Medically, however, dying is the final portion of human life. When does it begin?

It is no more possible for the observer to decide this exactly than it is possible for him to decide the moment of death. Dying can take seconds, minutes, hours, days. Lev Landau was dying for three months.[9] The doctor can often hold up the process of dying, delay it, even break it off altogether, so that death does not take place at all on that particular occasion. Medicine brings the dying person back to life. If we suffer from an incurable disease, we can be in bondage to death. Then we know for years that we are going to die, perhaps die 'soon'. All the same, that certainty and painful waiting is not dying.

Dying, rather, begins with the acute stage, what hospitals call the terminal phase. The doctor has seen that he cannot cure the patient. He can only try to make his sufferings bearable. That does not mean that he will not go on doing everything to fight the disease. But the goal of his efforts is now much more expressly the subject, the patient, as well as the object, the disease. This involves problems on both sides. The doctor and his helpers have come to the end of their resources. That is always a heavy burden. The whole hospital knows who the patient is that is dying. The patient usually knows it far sooner than he shows. Dying begins mentally and emotionally for him at the moment when he accepts that the time-limit is short, whether he accepts that fact in a positive or a negative way, or whether the two attitudes struggle for mastery within him. This coming to terms with the facts involves hard mental and spiritual labour.

But ways of dying differ greatly. As I said, one person may take a long time to die, another dies in a second, a third seems to have no death at all, as it were. A body can be shattered and torn to pieces through a fall, an accident, or an enemy shot, without the person's experiencing the act of dying at all in the real sense. 'He dropped dead', says the report. But all the same we still say 'he died'. He died without ever being able to say: I am dying. This sudden dying, which reaches its goal at the very moment when it sets out to seek it and which is the equivalent of death itself, used to be feared as the worst thing that could happen to a person—at all periods which refused to elevate superficial life into an ideal. This is contrary to the fear which people generally have of dying.

A person challenges this fear by telling himself that something essential is being taken from him when experience of the final hour is snatched away. It even used to be continually maintained that the final hour was life's most important hour in general. To take it away from someone is therefore as good as robbing him of the fulfilment of his life's significance. In the framework of this thinking, to call dying a process seems too colourless. Is dying not more an activity on the part of the dying person? Language indicates this as well. It uses an active verb: I die, not, I am died. It can even use a transitive verb: I die my own death. Language thinks of a purpose-

ful activity proceeding from the dying person, a process in the sense
of a pro-ceeding, a going forward, a going on.

Something goes *on* inside the mind of the dying person. But the
dying person also goes *towards*, proceeds towards something in the
act of dying. Our modes of dying do not only differ because of the
medical reasons for dying. We are different as people. My own
death is the expression of my own particular and unique life, and
among all the reasons for death, one is the most singular and most
wilful. No statistics include it. There are doctors who do not recognise it. Others cite countless credible testimonies of it and the
experience of centuries makes it indisputable: a person can die of a
broken heart.

In cardiac hospitals the factors leading to coronaries are listed
with punctual regularity as a warning: diabetes, high blood-
pressure, stress, nicotine. But no-one can say why someone breaks
down on that particular day and why another doesn't, in spite of all
kinds of damage. Why does a mother die when her son doesn't
come home? She dies because he doesn't come home. But why?
The post-mortem finds no explanation for a lot of things. The
anatomist is often unable to say why, in the case of this particular
illness, death should take place at that particular moment; and the
cause is often totally inexplicable. We have names to cover up this
obscurity, but we really know nothing at all.

The reason is not simply that the methods of contemporary medical science are apparently not sufficient to explain the correlation
between cause and effect in every case. It is rather that we do not
sufficiently realise that, in most of the cases where sudden dying
and death is not caused by external circumstance, the death, like the
illness, involves the human mind or soul and is partly—indeed
often solely—caused by it. Almost every death proceeds from the
mind. According to one view, even what we call the 'natural
causes' of death—the wear and tear on our organs through life-long
use—proceed from the mind. Actually it is not difficult to follow
this argument, since the psychological factors involved in the age-
ing process are obvious. One person with a feeble body will stay
alert for decades longer than many others who are bursting with
health, simply because he has the will to live, the courage to carry

out important jobs or functions, the power of spiritual renewal, faith, and confidence.

People can literally die of fear. Criminals have dropped dead before their execution. Oppressive feelings of guilt have led to death. Failure in one's job, monotonous work, boredom, or a joyless existence lead to illness and premature death; the high early death-rate among retired civil servants has been statistically proved. Where hope seems no longer capable of fulfilment, the readiness of the mind to admit deadly disease into the body grows. Suicide can be viewed as the extreme instance of this readiness. Conversely, hope can keep a person from dying and can even save him after the dying process has actually begun. Today we are beginning to investigate these correlations, but we are still far from giving therapeutical weight to the reality of the mutual interactions of body and mind and to the immense importance of mental factors in the process of illness and dying.

Death: the Medical View

In dying (as I believe and as I read in convincing reports given by people who have gone through the process of dying) the mind or soul not infrequently goes ahead. In this sense dying is for me a pro-ceeding or process. But the doctor thinks of this process in the sense of 'something going on', with a beginning, definite ascertainable phases, and, finally, life's unavoidable issue into its negation, death. He wants to, and has to, find out what the 'something' is that is going on there. He sees a pathological process reach the stage in which the person is merely the sufferer, i.e., loses his freedom of decision, because the disease is absorbing all the organism's energies. The patient visibly loses the quality of 'selfness'—or so the people round him think they can perceive; he increasingly becomes pure 'object', until he becomes for us wholly object, in death.

Medicine calls dying the process in which the integrity, the wholeness, and the unity of a person disintegrates. Consciousness counts incontestably as the sole criterion of this disintegration. The process is said to lead to the irretrievable loss of consciousness. The vegetative activities which determine human life gradually stop:

breathing, pulse, brain. Of these three, the activity of the brain counts in medicine today as being the most important criterion for the termination of life and the point when dying passes into death. The individual's death counts as established today when the electro-encephalograph no longer records wave patterns, or currents, in the brain. People cannot survive the failure and loss of other organs as well, such as the lungs, liver, and kidneys. Still, we have already learnt how to replace the kidneys for long periods, and the heart for shorter ones; and circulation and the heart can be revived. But wherever the damage may be, a person's death always ultimately takes place in the brain.

For the brain cells disintegrate immediately they cease to have blood supplied to them, the part of the brain which is most important being in fact the quickest to decay. The brain stem (or *truncus cerebri*), however, is not so important a factor for the occurrence of the death which the doctor establishes as the *cerebrum*, which only man possesses and which is probably the seat of our consciousness. In the medical sense, therefore, a person dies of the organ which marks him out as being human and a living organism. Doctors and positivist philosophy agree that someone's life is finished when he is no longer conscious of living.

However, we shall be testing what this means and what it does not mean against accounts given by the dying themselves. We shall then also have to ask the fundamental question, what the consciousness really is, and how it changes in dying. But first of all it must be said that we cannot in any case be content with such simple information; for both concepts, the concept of life and the concept of consciousness, are cloudy general terms, which only yield up their true substance when we develop them. Thus there are writers who maintain that the consciousness is snuffed out in sleep (which the peoples of the ancient world after all called 'a little death'); other people say, with reason, that this is far from being the case. But everyone is bound to admit that when we are asleep we are hardly aware, at least, of being alive. According to the definition above, therefore, we would be dead when we are sleeping. It would be truer to say that in sleep, in a still unexplained way, our consciousness conquers other, unknown territories. This is also true of dying, as we shall see; but here again this is the case in a quite different way from dreaming. Moreover it seems that the work of the human consciousness in dying is dependent on the mode of dying and the reason for it.

The concept of nature finds its limits in man. That is why a person's death can never be a natural death in the strict sense of the word. Unmoved by this discussion, the doctors still divide dying broadly, first of all, into natural and unnatural death, i.e., into unavoidable 'natural' death from old age (which human destiny imposes on us) and avoidable, or at least deferrable, 'unnatural' death through accident and disease. But Montaigne held precisely this type of death to be the natural one, since it is far and away the most frequent, and considered that the other (death through old age) was unnatural. In this he has been proved correct even in today's age of high life expectancy. For in actual fact, in western countries, almost no-one, medically speaking, dies of old age any more. The figure given today for West Germany, for example, is less than 20,000 a year, which is less than 3% of all deaths. The fact is that the better a country's medical care is, the seldomer 'death from old age' is given as a diagnosis; for today it counts as being the mark of medical ignorance. Even the old die of some illness or other; that is to say, according to the medical view they die of an avoidable accident of nature, i.e., unnaturally. And the doctors hope to be able to prevent many more illnesses in the future than is already the case today.

How far can they prolong life? Where would life's natural limit then lie? Speculation knows no bounds. But today serious ethical questions already stand in the way of unlimited medical advance, and not least in the light of our present subject. If dying has after all quite different aspects from the ones the outsider can see—and, as far as dying is concerned, the doctor is an outsider too—then we should also have to talk differently about natural and unnatural death, and about the prolongation of life.

Dying Anonymously

Our era goes in fear of its life. We discover this once again in the way we banish illness, as the sign of our mortality, into the hospital, and death into the hospital's wards for the dying. Anyone who has ever been in a hospital, or still more in an intensive care unit, has found that there above all the subject of dying and death is avoided, benevolently and persistently, though this is the last place where one might expect this avoidance. Here death is ubiquitous, but it is concealed as cunningly as possible. The world of the modern hospital, which after all has to deal with death every day, is radiant in festal white, and here the initiated only talk about death in Latin, as if it belonged to a past age. The people beside me in the ward, all four of them, who in the morning didn't come back from the rooms for the dying, night having closed in for them, were cheated of their deaths one by one in these eight weeks. We shall be talking about the way this happens.

Dying belongs to the very midst of my life. I experience it mentally. But when I have it in front of me in its clearest form, physically experienced, I turn away from it or don't face it honestly. It is not only the sick and the people who look after them who have difficulty in talking about the death which is going to be accomplished there in hospital; visitors have equal difficulty. We only have to see, from the next bed, the families as they arrive in their Sunday best, their arms full of flowers which only make work for the nurses, and on all their faces, fresh from the open air, the same smiles, which announce to father that now everything is soon going to be all right. Perhaps, now that his foreboding has become an imperative certainty, he has developed the shy and unusual wish finally to come to the point with those belonging to him: to sum up this long life of theirs together and to say some worthwhile word that will mean more and last longer than a photograph. But they don't break through his isolation; they chat and ask what the food is like. And even later, when they come one by one, only whispering now because things are serious, they seldom succeed in breaking the spell cast by society: one doesn't talk about these things. We want dying to be anonymous; that is to say, we do not want to give it a name, to express it in words.

The dying person himself is under the same spell too. Now he only has gestures for it. A veiled word, which they do not understand. 'How the blackbird is singing!' he whispers. But he means: 'This is probably the last time.' And, since he knows what his condition is, he wants to talk about his death. But he will hardly allow his doctor to break through the sound barrier behind which his soul is suffering—he is even unwilling to let his priest or pastor do so. Perhaps the other person, who is still in the midst of life, knows more about what dying really is than I do, though I am face to face with it—that other person, who is the custodian of the mystery, as they say. Hasn't life a single word that I can take with me into the act of dying?

The dying person would like to think so. But the barrier is there. The thing isn't given its name. They circle round the person when they know 'it' about him, as if he is someone who now deserves the best treatment in the hospital. It is touching; it is as if people had to make up to him for dying. The only thing they just cannot do is to tell him the truth. They talked about this for a long time during their training, discussing the fact that the nurses are forbidden to tell him; and the doctor talks in technical Latin terms, as we have said.

As long as life throbs within us, we deny ourselves to death. That is why we view the 'terminal patient' like a person who is just going to be executed, although he is innocent.

> Every hospital visitor feels superior to the person who is fatally ill, in a thoroughly base way. Do what you like, in the depths of your soul something like triumph will well up. For you are alive, you are going to go on living, and the person over there is going to die. Even though you repress your feeling of superiority, even though you are ashamed of it and curse it, it will show itself in your face and your demeanour.[10]

Then, as the end draws near, when 'it' is just ahead, people will avoid the sick person. Earlier, the dead counted as being unclean. Are the dying unclean today? This person here, the dying person, the object of medical failure, already belongs to the other side, the one we shun. His surroundings are sterilised, disinfected, neutralised, the mortuary is prepared. The desire to keep away from him spreads more and more, even though unexpressed by anyone, not admitted by anyone, even in his heart of hearts.

Lawrence LeShan timed this in a New York hospital. It emerged that the nurses and orderlies took longer to answer a patient's bell the nearer he was to death. They were not in any way acting maliciously; they were not even conscious of the way they were behaving.[11] They were only showing what power the dread that hangs over the process of dying and over dying people exercises, even in the case of people who have undertaken to nurse them.

Man is the being who has a name and who gives names to the world. Now he is dying, namelessly, without words, seldom waking to speech from the poisoned state to which medication has reduced him. That means dying an inhuman death. Out of five people, society lets four go through their final hour in hospitals and geriatric nursing homes. Parish priests and ministers in West Germany declare that they are called to someone who is dying at home only twice or three times a year at most.[12] Everyone has to get over this dying business all by himself.

The Signs of Death

The doctor has done what he can for his 'terminal patient'. Then he retreats. He has read the writing which does not deceive him. The nurse has been given her instructions. She may stay with the patient. She may call the relatives. But then it all goes so fast. She shuts the door more quietly than usual. The dying person shows 'the signs of death', we say. We know that these signs herald the end, but we do not comprehend them. We only see that the dying person is turning into a stranger. He seems completely withdrawn. He already belongs to 'another world', as we say. The difficult thing is: he has not yet left this world, but he has already ceased to be at home in it. Hovering between life and death, he is moving towards death in a movement which can no longer be stayed. What is the special world of the dying? It is only when we know more about this intermediate region that we can say more about dying itself.

There are differences. We see dying people who apparently

accept what is happening to them, so peaceful are their faces. Is it weariness, resignation, giving up? We see others who deny themselves to death. There is rebellion in their faces. Their hands are clenched over the bed cover. Is it defiance, rebellion, fear?

We should like to think so. For we have often heard it said that death causes fear, that dying is something infinitely terrifying, an anticipation of all the evil that comes afterwards: judgement, purgatory, hell: who knows? or heaven: who knows? And the uncertainty! On whom should it weigh more heavily than on the dying? Mustn't the same things be going on in his mind as in this man's, in the following account?

> The black masses of earth begin to slip on top of me. Without meaning to, in a second I lift my spade up and bore it into the earth in front of me, in frantic fear. I squat down, and with the help of my arm and the spade succeed in hollowing out a little opening in the black mountain that has fallen on top of me. Stiff and rigid, I watch over this little opening; all my limbs are pinned down ... buried, buried! The opening gets narrower and narrower, the wall is closing in, my back bends slowly under the frightful pressure of the mass of earth, my limbs are getting cramped ... everything in me seems to be being torn to pieces. I am on the verge of going mad ... [13]

May it not always be like this? The account of this man who was buried alive corresponds to the idea which very many people have of dying: life will be forcibly crushed out of us, hope will dwindle, fear will become more and more compulsive, resistance more and more useless, the darkness more and more pitiless; we shall lose our reason until it is all finished, until we are lost. And so the dying person lying in bed in front of us already belongs to his own world, a world unknown to us, in which he is for us entirely withdrawn and alien.

But many people have reported what happened after they had had an accident or had gone through a near-fatal illness, not only this man who was buried alive. These are rare and valuable accounts, for two things must coincide before they can come into our hands: the dying person must be saved from death, he must 'come to himself' again, as we say; and, secondly, he must be able and willing to talk about it. Today, in numerous cases that would once have ended in death, modern medicine can literally reanimate patients, even when the process of dying has already begun; just as it was always possible to use artificial respiration on the drowned, even after they had already appeared to be dying. But only few people can formulate in words what they experienced during this period, and most of them do not like to talk about it, for reasons which we shall hear later. These are highly intimate experiences, so incredible that those involved expect only a few people to believe them, and so personal that they are only unwillingly divulged.

Writers have tried again and again to grasp imaginatively this mystery of dying. All literature that strives after the depths reaches towards this dimension, where man touches his limits. Shakespeare's kings and heroes almost always die their great deaths crushed by a tragic destiny. The final words of the dying have for poets a higher degree of truth and vision than anything they say in life. The final curse, the final blessing are legitimated by the divine proximity into which the dying person is now entering. In Faust, Goethe makes Valentin, Gretchen's brother, deal with the matter in heroic brevity and spontaneous faith:

A soldier good, full well I know
That through death's sleep to God I go.[14]

Rainer Maria Rilke, to give only one example, presented the death of the Danish chamberlain Christoph Detlev on Ulsgaard as the vision of a deadly power which transforms the dying person into a wordless cry, so to speak. What happens to friends, neighbours, servants, and dogs, imperiously and horribly, during the ten weeks when Detlev's death 'dwells' on Ulsgaard reveals itself as being the outward appearance of the work of dying on the soul. The dying of this mighty man tyrannises the whole house. He dies as he has lived: evilly, greatly, capriciously, without patience and demanding the end.[15]

We should like to see this in outward terms: that what happens when we die is an echo of the way we have lived. For no longing is so strong in us as the longing for a squaring of accounts. This may be the spiritual side of the Freudian equalisation of the drives. We so much want to see ourselves rehabilitated through the rehabilitation of the world, and that means primarily other people. 'All the evil we do will come home to roost on earth, and inevitably in the hour of death' is an old dogma of popular faith. The Danish clergyman Hans Martensen–Larsen found it again in the account of a man who claimed to have experienced this vengeance in his own soul when he was dying (a death from which he was afterwards rescued).[16] If we were God, this is how we should arrange things: a person must pay the penalty for what he has done. That is why a wicked man (like Rilke's Danish chamberlain) also has to have a wicked death. Taking this a step further, we should admittedly have to say that since there is no-one who has not also done evil things during his life (since we all, measured against an ultimate standard, have failed in the task committed to us in life) every dying person is bound to know the bitterness of the work of vengeance. The person who is dying is standing before his judge, says popular belief. That is why he becomes increasingly remote from us.

Is Dying Quite Different?

We have seen what dying looks like from the outside, what death means in our society today, and what we think awaits us when we confront it. But this is country in which everything that we see can be deceptive and all the opinions that we form can be mistaken. We only grasp the negative side of dying, because we are still in the midst of life.

Stricken by what we have lost, we see in death deprivation and loneliness. We, who want to have and to possess, understand dying as deficiency, whereas it may perhaps mean freedom. The dying person leaves our space and our time. We cannot judge at all what this brings him. Indeed even the word 'leaves' is inappropriate.

All the basic facts of our life are ambivalent in kind. Work fulfils and fatigues, play refreshes or distracts, fire warms and burns, our very birth was both helplessness and joy. Is it not possible that dying too either crushes or liberates us, and that death destroys or exalts?

Everything within us resists dying. But we struggle just as vigorously against the idea that dying might be quite different from what we have always been told and from what we have always already suffered in anticipation in our willingness to accept life fully. For when all is said and done, we were shaken by fear, we felt ourselves threatened from all sides, family life was hell, as we said, we were cast down, depressed, we ran our heads against brick walls, strayed through dark tunnels; our loved ones died off one after the other, and the dreadful intelligence of the imminent death of mankind through radiation and nuclear power took our breath away like Job's messengers of gloom; we wept over graves; the heavens fell. Yes, this is just what dying will be like, one day, we tell ourselves.

But it is not true. Dying leads us out of the life in which all this happens every day. Its meaning and its reality is an expansion of our existence. One could fill books with the voices of writers and philosophers, devout men and women of all ages, who talk about this reality of their visionary faith. The religious mysticism of all eras has talked about it in tones that cannot be ignored. In our own day too it defines the meaning of dying as penetration into a reality which we certainly cannot see but which is not therefore nothingness, not dead, not insusceptible to our spirits:

> When I feel I am losing hold of myself and am absolutely passive within the hands of the great unknown forces that have formed me; in all those dark moments, O God, grant that I may understand that it is You (provided only my faith is strong enough) who are painfully parting the fibres of my being in order to penetrate to the very marrow of my substance and bear me away within Yourself.[17]

Any one of us who dares to say a word more about death and dying than Epicurus, Darwin, Marx, and Freud have said is already talking theologically. Epicurus, in the fourth century B.C., thought that there was nothing to be said about death at all: 'It does not concern us, since in death body and soul lose their capacity for sensation.'[18] We all continually say more than that. That is what men and women are like. And they owe it to themselves.

This book is an attempt at a new approach. It does not aim to speculate about dying, but to let the dying speak for themselves. Perhaps they can enrich what we have to say about dying and death through their experience? These experiences do not take us into the region of faith. We are only tunnelling a little further along the shaft in which we work at what we can actually know. More questions will confront us than we can find answers for. We can overvalue these experiences; on the other hand many a reader will say that our conclusions do not go far enough. We can interpret them wrongly; and other readers will say: why draw on experience at all? After all we have revelation, which gives us certainty in any case.

Shrinking from the subject, but deeply affected by what I had heard, I gathered together the accounts of people who, having once entered on the process of dying (or having almost completed it), then returned to everyday consciousness. There have always been lucky cases when people have returned like this. If today (as critics say) the return of the dying and the dead in the intensive care units of our great hospitals is organised by 'a medical mafia conforming to market trends', which sees dying and revival 'as a merely technical problem',[19] then this misuse of people is not my subject here. But we must no doubt reckon with the possibility that we shall have many more reports of this kind in the future than are given here.

What questions do these accounts raise for us?

3. DYING SEEN FROM WITHIN

The Escape of the Self in the Experience of Dying
We should have to give up our usual ideas about dying if it emerged
that, contrary to customary medical doctrine, the consciousness
does not end when we die. All the accounts which we have collected, however, suggest precisely this. They tell us about an extra-
ordinarily increased activity on the part of the consciousness in the
moments before death.

This activity is very varied in kind, just as every death has its
own character. But certain elements recur persistently, again and
again. I have chosen three: the escape, or exit, of the self; the
account rendered by the self, or the 'life panorama'; and the expansion of the self. In many accounts these three elements are clearly
distinguished from one another; in others they are intertwined; still
other reports include only one or two of these essential parts of the
activity of dying. We cannot maintain, either, that what is presented in the following pages is all that the consciousness accom-
plishes in dying. For to do that we should have to be able to
compare a great many more reports. But it seems to me probable
that we have discovered something important, and that dying tends
in this direction, even though what the dying person's consciousness achieves, its content, may differ.

Life offers many analogies for the first thing, the exit of the self;

this continually recurs when people who were dying and were then revived tell what they felt. Many people have experienced this: for instance under the laughing-gas anaesthetic that dentists used until recently. The experience was as follows:

> I was frightfully nervous until I was given the anaesthetic for the operation. For some time—I cannot remember any more for how long—I wasn't conscious of anything. Suddenly there was a heavy blow, which I resisted with my whole inner self. It seemed to me that I was going to be torn apart. But just as suddenly, immediately after the blow, everything was quiet: I saw myself lying there. I looked down from a floating position and saw a sharply defined picture of the operating table on which I saw myself lying, the operation wound on the right hand side of my body, the doctor with an indefinable instrument in his hand. I observed all this quite clearly. I tried to prevent the operation. I heard the words which—as they told me later—I apparently cried out: 'Stop! What are you doing?'[20]

Drug addicts also report that they experienced a split between body and soul of this kind, especially under the influence of hashish. But it does not seem to be dependent on narcotics. Children have experienced it, and adults who were in a completely 'sober' state. The liberation of the self in question seems to be aided not by any abnormal gift, but by certain mental conditions. It generally seems to be preceded by a clouding of the consciousness, however:

> The dizziness increased. But then my senses quickly cleared again. I was standing in the room and knew that I was separated from my body. My thoughts became acutely clear. I gave myself a complete account of my condition. I analysed my feelings and thoughts carefully, and was conscious of the fact that I was analysing them—I was even conscious of this consciousness itself. Although it was night, I saw everything clearly, but not quite in the way one perceives the daylight when one is awake ... I wasn't wearing any clothes ... I was standing up and was able to move, either walking or gliding over the floor. I saw my

body quite clearly, lying stretched out on the bed on its back, like a corpse.[21]

The person giving the account then describes his vain attempts to make his body move. Finally he woke up 'by means of auto-suggestion', 'gradually and without any shock', wrote down what he had gone through and then slept deeply for two hours.

Reports of this kind are by no means confined to periods in which spiritualism was widespread. They belong to the fundamentals of human experience and may well be only reported so seldom because they are so strange. For example, the Low German seventeenth-century mystic Hemme Hayen tells us:

... I was lying in bed, in the morning; it was already bright daylight and I was already fully awake. My mind lay in deep contemplation and in the rapture I thereupon experienced, my new man, as if side by side at my bedside, departed from the old one, leaving me lying on the bed like a dead log. Turning round, I therefore saw my natural body lying dead. But I myself came once again into dazzling light.[22]

This mystical experience coincides with the psychological knowledge of our own day. The modern reporter does not talk about a dead body and the *persona gloriae*, but it could well be that he saw the same thing. He saw an unscathed reality, which parted from a sick one. Reports given by the dying are close to mystical experience. In both cases it is a question of life and death. A down-to-earth person belonging to our own day, a policeman whom the doctors were able to revive, chose these simple words:

I was driving home late, after my evening spell of duty. Suddenly I found myself among some people who were standing round a car that had been involved in an accident. A girl was busy pulling a body out of the car. None of the others was lifting a finger. I think they were all paralysed by the shock of what had happened. And I thought: Why are you standing stock-still among all these onlookers? Then I was finally able to see the face of the person who had been involved in the accident: it was my own. Now the girl was kneeling over my body and I stood beside her, paralysed by shock, and looked on helplessly. The girl pressed her mouth to mine and began artificial respiration. Then I suddenly saw nothing more. The next thing I was conscious of was opening my eyes in hospital.[23]

There is apparently no time-limit for this personal schism in dying. An English account gives two hours:

I was in a hotel in London. I woke up in the morning feeling slightly unwell (I have a weak heart) and immediately afterwards I fainted. To my great astonishment I soon found myself in the top part of the room, from where I could see my lifeless body, in bed, with its eyes closed. I tried unsuccessfully to re-enter my body, and concluded from this that I was dead. I began to wonder what the hotel people and my relatives and friends would say. I asked myself whether there would be an inquest and how my business affairs would now be settled. I had certainly lost neither my memory nor my self-consciousness. I saw my lifeless body as if it had been some separate object; I was able to look at my face. But I couldn't leave the room. I felt as if I were chained up, confined to the corner where I was. After one or two hours I heard someone knock several times at the locked door; but I wasn't able to give any sign of life. A short time afterwards, the hotel door-keeper appeared on the balcony, to which a fire escape led up. I saw how he entered the room, looked nervously at my body and then opened the door. Soon the hotel manageress and other people came in. A doctor arrived. I saw him shake his head as he listened to my heart and then forced a spoon between my lips. I lost consciousness and woke up in bed. All this lasted at least two hours.[24]

This extremely long dissociation phase contrasts with others which can only have lasted for seconds, according to the report of outsiders and the consciousness of the dying person himself. In these cases the person is apparently extremely astonished later at how much bewildering and liberating experience his consciousness could absorb in this short time, in lightning speed, as it were. We shall be hearing more about this. In *Seele und Tod* ('The Soul and Death', 1934) Jung wrote about this: 'An objective examination and criticism of existing observations allows us to establish that perceptions take place which partly come about as if there were no space and partly as if there were no time.' We are already familiar with this phenomenon from our own dreams. When we wake up we think that it is so difficult to put the dream into our own words because words demand a logical progression, whereas the dream conveyed all its images to us at the same moment, as it were. And this although we none the less think that we have been tormented or delighted by an apparently endlessly long succession of dream experiences.

In the same way our dreams have often familiarised us with the idea that not only can many things happen simultaneously, but that we ourselves can also be in many places simultaneously. The process of dying confronts us with the same problem in its first phase and stratum. Yet the experiences people have while dying are not dreams. We shall be confronted with the difference again and again. Here, in this initial experience, the exit of the self, which is common to all these accounts of dying, the difference appears in the fact that the dying person does not give an account of a multiplicity of shifting phantasmagoria. On the contrary, our reports continually present merely two versions.

The one implies that the escaping self preserves a particular and apparently constant distance in space from the body of the dead person. It often feels fixed, 'chained up in the corner'.[25] It often finds itself, to its astonishment, in 'an elevated place'.[26] The distance is sometimes given quite precisely: 'I was floating in the air about ten feet up',[27] 'about ten to thirteen feet horizontally over the bed'.[28] The escaping self has been assigned a position in space. From there it observes the body it has left behind, which is always described as being dead, lifeless, or limp, and is at least incapable of perception itself.

The other group of accounts says that when the self leaves the body it moves freely in space and even outside the dying person's

room. And whereas in the other reports the escaped self only perceives nearby things—'oneself down there', the site of the accident,
the operation process—in these it acquires an unhindered view of
wider perspectives. The dissociated self is quite conscious of its
freedom.

> I was standing in the centre of the room and plainly saw my dead
> body lying on the cot. I started to leave the room and met one of
> the doctors. I wondered that he did not say something to me,
> but as he made no effort to stop me I went out into the street
> ... and there met an old acquaintance, M. B. I attempted to
> strike him on the back by way of salutation, but my arm passed
> right through him. . . . I utterly failed to attract his attention. I
> distinctly saw him walk across the street and gaze at a miniature
> Ferris wheel in a window. . . . I went up to the hospital to see the
> body. I passed through the door and gazed at myself for a time. I
> ... heard the doctors discussing my case. One of the specialists
> wanted to try some experiment with a new electrical apparatus.
> The instruments were attached to my feet and I distinctly felt the
> sensation while standing in the centre of the room.[29]

The reporter states that he possesses letters and telegrams showing that M.B. was in the town on that particular day, walked down
that street, and looked at the little Ferris wheel in the window.

In the most severe phase of typhoid, the doctor A.S.W. was
without pulse and perceptible heart-beat for an hour. He was
declared dead. According to his own account, however, he himself
believed that he was unconscious for a time, but then came to his
senses again, as 'his true self', but still within the body whose
anatomical marvels he observed with a doctor's interest. Then his
account goes on:

> I realised my condition and reasoned calmly thus. . . . I have
> died ... and yet I am as much a man as ever. . . . I watched the
> interesting process of the separation of soul and body. . . . As I
> emerged, I saw two ladies sitting at my head. I measured the
> distances between the head of my cot and the knees of the lady

opposite the head and concluded there was room for me to
stand.... I seemed to be translucent, of a bluish cast and
perfectly naked. I ... saw my own dead body. I was surprised
at the paleness of the face. I saw a number of persons sitting
and standing about the body, and particularly noticed two
women apparently kneeling by my left side.... I have since
learned that they were my wife and my sister.... I now
attempted to gain the attention of the people but found that
they gave me no heed.... I concluded the matter by saying to
myself: '... They are watching what they think is I, but they
are mistaken. That is not I. This is I and I am as much alive as
ever.'

I turned and passed out at the open door ... into the street.
There I stopped and looked about me. I never saw that street
more distinctly than I saw it then. I took notice of the redness of
the soil and of the washes the rain had made.[30]

In the accounts of some of the people who have gone through the
process of dying, we find indications, on the other hand, that they
now perceive their different, observing and reflecting self as being
in a strange form. We heard in the last account that it was 'transparent, blueish in colour'. Other people find it difficult to discover an
appropriate word. 'I wasn't wearing any clothes on my fluid body.'
Others claim that, as they kept watch in the room of the dead
person, they saw from outside their 'astral body' above the corpse,
according to an English account in the form of a deep purple cloud
of smoke.[31]

The reports are unanimous in saying that the escaped self was
itself perceptible, but that it possessed no bodily appearance. 'My
hand went right through the middle', we hear again and again.
Doors offer no resistance, distances have little meaning. Gravity
seems to be abolished. The exit of the self is experienced as liberation. There are patients who are able to describe the process of
dying in all its phases. As a psychic experience, the beginning looks
roughly as follows:

The consciousness was strangely calm and clear. I was no longer in pain.... Gradually the consciousness, which normally suffuses the whole body, became condensed in the head. I became all head, and only head. Then it seemed that 'I' had become condensed into one tiny speck of consciousness, situated somewhere near the centre of my head.... Then I became aware that I was beginning to travel further upwards. There came a momentary blackout and then 'I' was free; I had left my body. I had projected in space somewhere above the bed upon which still lay my inert body. And I knew—this is what the world calls the state of death.[32]

Let us sum up what has been said up to now in these reports given by people who, once having died, were able to talk about it afterwards. The initial stage of dying seems to them like an awakening. They find that their consciousness is intensified. It is drawn together, perhaps in the head, or at a particular point in the head. The authors of the reports maintain that they were calm, collected, and lucid, when they suddenly saw themselves confronted with the conviction of being outside their bodies. The first phase of the exit of the self then seems to begin with the self's staying near the body, but elevated above it. The self observes its own body and its nearby surroundings from the outside, without interest and without regret. Then the self retreats from its body, attempts to leave it, reaches the open. We shall hear from other accounts that, having left the body, the self tries to find another reality or soon finds itself in one. In some cases a strange, new bodily state was experienced, weightless and full of light. There seems to be capacity for objective observation, but the capacity to communicate or to exert an influence on things is limited. According to everything that we shall hear presently, the exit of the self is only the first step which the dying person takes and is the pre-condition for everything else that he experiences afterwards.

But we must be clear about the fact that the escape of the self, emphatically stressed though this usually is, is by no means only a matter of the spatial experience of a bodily detachment that could be gauged by tape measures. It is true that this phase of dying is generally experienced as the being above (and probably also the being fixed to) a point not far away. But the exit or escape of the self has a goal, and yet has none; it is a 'where to' and yet not a 'where to'. It is at least always an escape in feeling and in mind, a local and at the same time an emotional removal from physical actuality. Perhaps even what we have in the accounts is merely the later translation of emotional experience into a spatial one by the author of the account, who is seeking after linguistic images whereby to translate into the everyday world the impression that eludes our logic, which also means our linguistic capacity. How often do our informants tell us that they can find no words and concepts for it. Words, they think, can only penetrate the forecourts of what they attained. They cannot even make it comprehensible to themselves, and the most strenuous efforts only allow them at first to lay hold of a world of pictures, though this certainly seems to them precise and clear. Then they fall silent, dazed and deeply affected. They know they have experienced something without parallel, but no-one can accept it or ought to accept it. Fear of talking about it prevails. Perhaps, only after weeks have gone by, they may touch on it and pass on the ideas that they formed in the meantime; and we can only express ideas in words. At the same time there are other people who, after their 'return' to everyday consciousness, open their eyes and immediately begin to tell their story: 'I was in another country.' Were they not so far away after all, since they can immediately find words for their experience? Is their account more superficial, or more immediate, than the one which could find formulation after a long space of time? We do not know.

The language of the medieval visionaries gives the name 'translation' to the state we call here the 'exit' or escape of the self. We have numerous accounts which allow us to make a comparison. And some of them give accompanying circumstances which allow us to conclude that what is being described is in reality an alteration of the consciousness in dying. For instance, we are told in the account of the vision of the Irish abbot Furseus, round about 650, that his experience took place during a severe illness. When he fell ill, Furseus asked to be taken home. But before he got there, he felt his legs being overcome by paralysis. He felt that he was sinking into darkness and was carried into the next house 'as one dead'.

'As one dead' he is translated. 'He sees four hands stretching out
to him out of the darkness' and, at first slowly, recognizes in the
darkness, in shadowy form, the shining figures of three angels,
who begin to escort him. But finally one of them commands
that Furseus should be taken back to his body. Only then does
Furseus notice that he is separated from his body. He asks his
companions where they are taking him. The angel on his right
answers that he must put on his own earthly body once more.
But Furseus is so charmed by the company of the angels that it
seems to him cruel anguish to have to return to his body again;
and he explains to the angels that he does not want to leave them
any more. Thereupon the angels command him to return to his
body, but promise him, as a consolation, that after the earthly
span allotted to him has been completed, they will fetch him
again ... Then his soul returns to his body again 'without being
able to say how it happened'. Furseus wakes up and hears the
laments of the funeral congregation, who have come to his burial. His friends are amazed and hurry to free his face from the
shrouds covering it. The same happens the following night.
Once more, already paralysed, he expects immediate death.
Again he is 'translated'. Again he sees the angels, and again he
experiences his return to the body as being especially laborious.
This time a demon molests him on the way, leaving burns on his
shoulder and face which will be seen later. The angels carry him
on to the roof of his church. And from here, at this fixed distance, he looks miraculously through the roof and the walls and
sees his naked body lying, forsaken by the soul. He is overcome
by fear of this strange body and refuses emphatically to go near
it. Only when the angel promises that he will enter his body
without suffering and that he, the angel, will come again to fetch
him, does Furseus agree. He sees how the body is opened at the
breast in order to let him in again. He 'then awakes in his body as
from a profound sleep of death and sees round him the company
of kinsmen, neighbours and clerics who have arrived in the
meantime.' Respiration and heart-beat begin again.[33]

We find another variant of our theme in the narrative of the English Presbyterian minister L.B. He had left his group when climbing a mountain and sat down exhausted on the edge of a precipice. According to his account he was suddenly attacked by paralysis, which was so severe and so sudden that he was not even able to throw away the match with which he wanted to light his cigar. It burnt his fingers. He noticed that his feet and hands were growing numb, then his knees and elbows, trunk, head; and finally the moment came when life 'departed'. He thought that he was dead and was conscious 'of floating in the air like a kind of balloon'. 'Looking down, I was astonished to recognize my own, deathly pale body. How curious, I said to myself, there is my body, in which I lived and which I called my self, as if the coat were the body and the body the soul ...' He saw the cigar in the corpse's hand, and imagined what his friends would say when they found his body. Then he perceived that they had chosen a route to the top of the mountain which they had expressly agreed not to take. And he saw the guide stealing food out of his friends' rucksacks. And then the minister recognized his wife. 'Hallo', he said, 'there's my wife going to Lungern, although she told me that she wouldn't leave until tomorrow.' Finally he felt himself being drawn downwards into his body, fell into 'confusion and chaos', in complete contrast to his clarity before, and, when he became fully conscious, found that his friends had found him and 'revived' him. He reproached them with breaking their word, and the guide with stealing. The man thought it was the devil, forewent his fee and ran away. What B. had seen with regard to his wife also proved correct.[34]

At this point we ought to stand back a little. What we have read has fairytale features. They make us sceptical. There seems to be every opportunity for deception. What degree of 'truth' can these stories claim? Simply the truth of a confession of faith. We cannot check them. Is it not perhaps possible that, in spite of their assurances to the contrary, these people of former times and our own day were dreaming, in the twilight zone between dying and death, between falling asleep and the re-awakening of the consciousness? To the objection that, when all is said and done, it is remarkable that they should all claim to have experienced the same thing or at least similar things (after all, they all claim to have undergone the 'escape of the self' first of all), the sceptic would object that it is quite possible for people of similar tendencies to follow in their 'dreams' a pattern which they had heard about some time or other in their lives. This is simply the way they had always imagined dying: body and soul are separated from one another. This is the pattern of Platonic philosophy: the soul's imprisonment in the body, from which death liberates it. This has been the popular belief from time immemorial of most religions, including Christianity: the soul leaves the body at death, perhaps in the form of a bird, or a butterfly, or a cloud of smoke, or a homunculus. Jung collected examples of this and interpreted them.[35] In death the son is born in the form of the soul and rises from the body in new spiritual form. Do we not have the vivid phrase 'he expired', i.e., breathed out? If the window of the death chamber is not opened, if the tile on the roof is not loosened, the soul remains imprisoned and shows itself next morning as a little blueish cloud of smoke. This has been 'folk' wisdom since the days of the Germanic tribes. In sleep or in ecstasy, the soul leaves the body and appears as a 'doppelgänger' in another place. Popular belief thinks of the spirit of the dead as being the soul, which has been split off and discarded in dying and now wanders round in sometimes visible form (as a spirit 'coming back from the dead' or a vampire), intervening in the lives of the living. Countless ancient burial customs served, and still serve, to ward off this being from the world beyond the grave, who is bent on injury and revenge. Since the days of the Romans one has not been supposed to speak ill of the dead; and this is the tamest of these defensive customs. We possess a wealth of naive representations in ancient ecclesiastical art, depicting dying as the escape of the soul. In these pictures, a miniature copy of the person is emerging from his dead body, generally out of his mouth—doll-like, smoky, sometimes with wings. This has its prototype in the Egyptian idea of the soul as a bird, and there is ample evidence for it in German folk sagas.

All this comes to mind when I hear accounts of the escape of the soul in dying. Could it not be the case that our informants are only presenting us with reminiscences of these primitive ideas? The wretched wandering souls of popular medieval theology, mankind's ancient notions about the transmigration of souls, animism, the incapacity of primitive people to distinguish between spirit and matter to conceive of the body in purely material terms and the soul in purely spiritual ones; the whole body-soul problem of philosophy and psychology—I am faced with all this in these accounts. Mustn't we consider everything afresh?

Here, right at the beginning of these accounts which we must face up to, shall I not already be thrown back on the question of who man really is? And what is reality, if a spiritual experience can be expressed like this? I have no desire to fall back on the blank cheque of all the people who fish in the murky waters of their ignorance, the much misused Shakespearean quotation:

There are more things in heaven and earth, Horatio,
Than are dreamt of in your philosophy.

Hamlet saw a poor soul who demanded revenge and got what he asked. His insight into the world of the dead remains on this side of the border. I do not believe that Shakespeare wanted to provide cover for spiritualism. For him, the fact that the dying migrate and the dead speak and that the soul has a future beyond the grave was a reality of faith that was much too much a matter of course for him to have felt forced to justify it—or for him to have wanted to do so. But his *Hamlet* saying is certainly not intended to mean that we should take at its face value all and everything that contradicts our experience.

Here, however, we have experience over against lack of experience. The accounts of the exit of the self in the phase when consciousness of the self is declining in unconsciousness and death are too numerous, too similar in form, and too unanimous for us to be able to shrug them off. Could we not equally well draw the opposite conclusion: that those folk beliefs preserve a submerged deposit of knowledge about true and important correlations, and that that is why similar features crop up in the reminiscences of the dying?

We will break off here in the hope that we shall gain more clarity when we turn to further reports, which take us beyond this first phase of dying, the exit of the self. The question remains: what kind of human consciousness is this, which arises when the consciousness linked with the brain cells is in the process of disappearing, or has already disappeared? Is it permissible for us to suppose that it is a bodiless consciousness? Modern men and women can only conceive of the soul as a principle, a *principium*, i.e., as the origin and basis of life in the body, in accord but also in interaction and a state of tension with it, and therefore always bound to the body. Is the soul now supposed to be able to acquire independence as a detached consciousness, invisible, intangible, a purely spiritual nature of a new kind and yet connected with the old one? Is the soul supposed to be able to preserve identity with itself, both within the body and outside it?

In earlier times people never doubted this. But for us these are new questions, and particularly suspect because they are such simple ones. For what is simple is for modern thinking the most difficult of all. We shall consider this again, after further accounts have spoken for themselves and have made us more clearly aware of the variety of dying experience. First of all, let us close this section with three accounts of the escape of the dying person's self.

All three examples are accident reports. The sudden threat to the person's life, the being abruptly overtaken by deadly peril, the extreme and unexpected strain put on the person's physical powers, drowning, freezing, falling, other accident—all these seem to give a person particular awareness of this sense of the exit of the self. One of the informants now speaking is remembering an accident he had when he was a boy. It was something that made a life-long impression on him. This report is interesting because it shows us only what happened, without any attempt at interpretation, and because we hear from it that even a child can experience the exit of the self in dying.

When he was eleven years old, W. had to clear away an electrical cable which a storm had torn down from its mast and thrown on to the road. When he picked up the wire, the high voltage immediately threw him to the ground and across the street. He lay there unconscious, without having been able to remove his hands from the wire. He hung on the wire for ten minutes and all the onlookers thought he was dead.

> I presently became conscious outside my physical body and saw it lying there ... I could feel the terrible electricity passing through me, even as I stood some feet away from my physical body, which was in contact with the wire. ... I could not move by my own volition. My arms, in the astral body, were held rigid—as if grasping a wire which was not there—just as my arms in the physical body were grasping a wire which *was* there. ...
>
> Amid this agony I could see the boys standing beside me, frightened dumb, but afraid to touch me (my physical body) lest they too became victims. In vain I shrieked to them to run for help, but they could neither see me in the astral body nor hear my pleas. Suddenly they seemed to gain their senses and began to shriek and jump about frantically.
>
> There I stood, helpless, for several minutes, which to me were like so many years. Then, thank God, I could see people coming on the run toward the spot, from all over the neighbourhood, and I seemed to know that someone would get me out of my torment. There was M. climbing a fence almost a block away, and he was one of my best friends. Over the fence I saw him come, then rush toward the scene.
>
> Two ladies from the nearby houses were coming. I knew them too. And there, a man and his son were running toward me—the man carrying a hatchet; he had rubber boots on. This man reached down to pick up my physical body, and as he did so, I seemed to bound right back into it again and was conscious there, as all the neighbours stood by, looking on. All were astonished at the fact that I 'came back to life,' as they said, and the examining physician who was called was likewise baffled.[36]

The Swiss architect S.v.J. passed on a detailed interpretation of his experience of dying, to which I shall come back later. He was thrown out of his car on 16 September 1964, and lay in the road unconscious, with eighteen broken bones. He calls the phenomenon which concerns us here (the exit of the self) 'a first intermezzo' in the process of dying.

I hovered over the site of the accident and saw my lifeless, badly injured body lying there, exactly in the position which I later found described in the police report. I also clearly saw our car and the onlookers. Then I noticed a man who was attempting to bring me back to life. I was able to hear what the people were saying. The doctor was kneeling on the right hand side, giving me an injection. Two others were holding me from the other side and were pulling off my clothes. I saw how the doctor forced my mouth open with a spatula and tried artificial respiration, and I heard him say: 'I can't give him cardiac massage, his ribs are broken.' Then he stood up and said—in funny Bernese German—'There's nothing to be done. He's dead.' People wanted to move my body away from the side of the road and asked the soldiers where there was a blanket to cover my body. I wanted to laugh, and to say to them, 'Don't make such a scene, folks; I'm not quite dead yet.' I found the whole thing rather funny, but it didn't worry me at all. I actually found it amusing to be able to look on at people's efforts. Then I saw someone in bathing trunks approaching, with a little bag in his hand. He talked to the doctor in standard German. He exchanged a few words with him, then knelt down beside me and did something to me. I was perfectly well able to fix the man's face in my mind. And in fact a man came into my hospital ward a few weeks later . . . I got a shock, for I knew at once that I had already seen him somewhere at some time or other. He said that he was the doctor who had given me the life-saving cardiac injection—I myself would say the 'devilish' injection, because it was with the injection that my sufferings began. I recognized him immediately and was even able to remember his voice quite well. We immediately became friends.

It was interesting to see this terrible scene, a man dying 'down there' after a car accident. What was especially interesting was that the man was myself and that I was able to observe myself exactly, from above, as an onlooker, without any emotion, quite calmly, in a heavenly, felicitous state, in 'divine harmony'. It is very seldom that a person sees himself dying. But it is more interesting still that this should happen without excitement and with the contented feeling: at last I'm dying. This was my first four-dimensional experience. I hovered about ten feet above the site of my accident. My sensory organs functioned; my memory was able to register everything. I wasn't conscious of any hindrance.[37]

For this informant (of whom we shall hear more later), the experience of dying becomes a religious one which changes him fundamentally and gives his life and thinking a new direction. He has to draw on the vocabulary of the east, to find order.[38]

I believe that during this time ... the silver cord still binding my astral body to my brain cakras became ever thinner and more elastic, like an astral umbilical cord. The moment approached when this silver thread was bound to snap like a rubber band under tension. This would have meant final death, following the clinical death which had long since taken place; that is to say, the whole process would have reached a threshold. Then there would no longer have been any possibility of a return from beyond.

I do not know how long it would have lasted before the silver cord snapped. According to earthly timekeeping, perhaps a few seconds or tenths of seconds remained, but in the fourth dimension, time and three-dimensional space stop. So I experienced this brief period of a few minutes and seconds during my clinical death as several days or several weeks, because I had experienced so much in this short time.

The Austrian writer Paul Anton Keller gives an account which speaks for itself of what he underwent after an accident. He was thirty years old when, together with other young men, he set up the maypole in his village. They levered the pole up, but the leafy crown which had been left was top-heavy and the pole fell on the narrator.

I had my eyes fixed on the crown. Suddenly I shivered, with an uncomfortable feeling of some immediately impending danger.

At that moment, in a second of crucial clarity, as my previous life merged into a single, abruptly outlined field of vision and became visible as a single whole, the crown snapped. There was a whistling and a rushing noise. I heard shouts. A frightful blow felled me to the ground. My body was twisted with pain. Then every noise faded. But no, I still heard, felt, saw, experienced and grasped the happening of the moment with a clarity and sense of release such as I had never experienced before in my living existence ... I saw myself, saw my body lying beside the hole on the trampled piece of meadow. A lump of clay stuck to my right temple. I noticed it clearly ... It was not only that I could see my familiar body, which lay there in the grass, covered with dirt, and which I observed with complete indifference, indeed almost with a feeling of sharpened aversion. I was concerned at the frightened gestures of my friends and the desperation of the teacher who, instead of the maypole, found a dying man on the grass in front of her window.

The doctor raced up on a bicycle. They lifted the body. Then I saw only the doctor's broad back as he bent over it. Still more inquisitive people came up. Someone had taken my coat from the doctor. The village hairdresser put it beside the rainwater butt. His hand slid into the top pocket and jumped dexterously back again. His fingers were clutched round my watch ... I caught his arm, but my grasp went right through, as if I were grasping at thin air. I joined the circle of gapers, feeling no resistance. I was astonished and confused, because the other people didn't see me, although I was more alive than ever before.

Suddenly I was standing beside the doctor. The waxen image of myself lay motionless in front of him. I felt moved by surprise that I should ever have been this thing, that this pallid body should somehow belong to me. The face with my features filled me with extreme repulsion because of its corpse-like colour. The hair was hanging dishevelled over the brow, one nostril was torn and bleeding profusely. The upper lip was drawn back. A twig was lodged between the exposed teeth; the teacher drew it out carefully with the tips of her fingers. The doctor filled the hypodermic. Not without curiosity, I saw him plunge it into the upper arm, neatly and yet carefully ... I was seized by an obscure fear, in which my feeling of complete calm was lost ... Then I was suddenly no longer able to recognize anything more in the external world.[39]

The Panorama of Life Experienced in Dying

The sense of the escape of the self seems to have ended with the doctor's injection. Apparently the resuscitated circulation conducted blood into other brain centres. Paul Anton Keller's report continues:

I drifted in marvellously pervaded interim regions, of which I was scarcely consciously aware and which I yet experienced with much more alert senses than it is given to dreamers and the mentally confused to do. I once more acknowledge the reality of what I experienced and maintain emphatically that I never at any other time in my life experienced the truest reality so clearly, down to the most factual intensification of what was felt. As for what happened to me afterwards: I should like to call it an awakening into clarity.[40]

In this clarity, time after time, the dying see appearing before them what psychology calls 'the life panorama'. Without being able to say what period of time is covered by this experience of their consciousness, they report (agreeing in many details) that their whole lives passed in front of their spirits, but in a remarkable review and selection of what had been most important, though they had never been conscious of this earlier. Let me give here the second part of the account, the beginning of which we have already heard.[41] The dying E.B. has just accepted that she is in the state 'that people call dead'. She then goes on:

Again a timeless pause and then before my inner sight there flashed a complete series of pictures embodying the most important events of my life. It seemed that I became both actor and witness in these pictures, for I found that with clear reason, utterly devoid of all prejudice or hazy emotion, I became my own judge of my own actions, for good or bad, throughout my preceding life. This judgment being over, there finally appeared to me only those people with whom there existed a true bond of love. And then I turned willingly and gladly to embark on this new life which was beginning for me.

The consciousness now gazes into the past, just as detachedly as it views the body which it has left. Different scenes belonging to former days emerge; the narrator suddenly now knows things that he could not possibly know. However we may care to evaluate this, the phenomenon of the life panorama is so frequently reported that we are bound to recognise it as being an important part of the process of dying.

It is often stressed (as we heard it stressed above by Paul Anton Keller) that this experience cannot be confused with a dream, because it possesses a closeness to reality which dreams never attain. In this experience, as it comes to the dying, it is not a question of ideas being lived as they are in a dream; on the contrary, it is life that is being thought and experienced. Above all, the consciousness of the self is completely different in kind from what it is in dreaming. The dreamer is incapable of putting himself in the place of a critical observer of the dream-happening, from whence he would be in a position to overlook every side of the situation. The dreamer experiences himself as part of the phantastic pictures; his consciousness of himself is direct, but not reflective. For the dying person it is vice versa: in this phase he sees himself in a position to judge himself, and continually talks of doing so. In sleep and in dream, on the other hand, our intention of keeping the processes of thought under control is hindered. It is only for that reason that the images can well up and take over control. It must at least be said that in dreams our self-control is reduced. We all know our own objection to the dream during the dream itself—the way we tell ourselves, even while we are dreaming, 'Oh, it's only a dream', so as not to let the impression made by the images gain too much power over us. But we only seldom make this objection in our dreams, and when we do, very fleetingly and unbelievingly. As a rule we surrender our selves while dreaming.

Moreover the dream-law of '*paranoira*' (the inclination, already recognised by the ancient Greeks, to observe things indirectly, not so much to show things as to refer to them, to indicate them, to circle round them, or to find a substitute for them) is totally alien to the experience of dying. Our accounts always talk about a directly viewed reality and a directly experienced closeness of the person's past life. Everything seems to the dying person as just what it is; everyone talks just as he had heard them talk in life. It is the selective imagination, not the creative one, that seems to have the upper hand here.

And the judging imagination. The dying person's life panorama evaluates. 'Between the stirrup and the ground', says the old epitaph, 'Mercy I sought, mercy I found': the rider who fell to his death lived through his spoilt life again, and found grace.[43] This is in line with what the dying tell us. A pious tale from Denmark makes the point in a few words:

A young fisherman from the west coast of Jutland wanted to dive into the water while bathing; but he hit his head on a stone and was drowning, having lost consciousness. He rose to the surface twice but went down again before he could be rescued. In these moments his whole life passed in front of him. First of all he felt completely deserted. Then he laid hold of God's grace and was drawn out again, a new man.[44]

Again and again, people (especially those who can tell of a swift, violent death) relate in astonishment with what extreme vividness the life panorama opens up before them. Many similar experiences, of a kind familiar to mountaineers, lie behind the account of the Austrian Hias Rebitsch. He was climbing the south face of the Goldkappel in South Tyrol, a rope-length ahead of his companions, secured by three pitons. An overhanging rock was still between him and his goal. He thought he had surmounted it, when a piton came loose and he fell backwards into the abyss in a break-neck drop:

I still grasp completely what is happening, am fully conscious of what is going on round me: I am brought up short for a moment. I register: the first piton has gone. The second. I strike against the rock, scrape against it as I go down, want to resist, to claw at it. But a wild power dashes me inexorably down and down. Lost. Finished.

But now I am not frightened any more. Fear of death leaves me. All feeling, every perception is snuffed out. Only more emptiness, complete resignation within me and night round about me. I am not plummeting downwards any more either. I am sinking softly through space on a cloud, resigned, released. Have I already passed the gateway to the kingdom of shadows? Suddenly light and movement enter the darkness round me. Cloudy figures detach themselves from me and become clearer and clearer. A film flickers on to a screen inside me: I see myself in it again, see myself, only three years old, tottering to the grocer's shop next door. In my hand I am clutching the penny that my mother had given me so that I could buy myself a few sweets. Then I see myself as an older child, see how my right leg is caught under a falling layer of planks. My grandfather is trying to raise the planks. Mother is cooling and stroking my crushed foot ... More and more pictures out of my life flicker up and are shaken into confusion. The film snaps. Chains of light cut through the empty black background like lightning. Catherine wheels, raining sparks, flickering will o' the wisps ... Again I am standing in front of myself. I cannot recognize myself physically in this form, but I know that it is me. Suddenly a cry out of the distance: 'Hias!' and again, 'Hias! Hias!' A call from within me? Suddenly sun-bathed rock and light and silence before me. My eyes have opened. The window into the past had been thrown open. Now it is shut again. And again the frightened cry. It comes from this world, from above ... Now I become conscious for the first time that I have just survived a great fall, have returned from a long journey, back through my life, back from an earlier existence, have slipped into my skin again. I worked myself up the seventy feet with the help of the rope ... The last piton had held.[45]

It is open to dispute whether shock reaction is subject to different physical laws from dying. There are doctors who explain fantastic experiences of this kind by saying that the fear of death causes the adrenal gland to produce and excrete hormones which have a similar effect to certain poisons, for instance hashish and LSD. We shall discuss this in detail later. But this report (which other mountaineers can parallel) seems to me to confirm the physical nature of dying. Although the climber was not organically injured in falling, he anticipated the experience of dying and experienced his 'life panorama'. He died psychologically, as it were, from his expectation of death, even though death never actually took place. In the same way, as Arthur Jores reports, it has been noticed at executions through the electric chair in America that some criminals are dead before the current is even switched on.[46]

Apart from the evaluating imagination of the life panorama, we quite often notice its liberating and redeeming character. It takes on this liberating, saving character by often presenting itself as a return home to the earliest past. The present disappears, the past becomes uncertain the further back it lies; but the very earliest past to be experienced at all rises up in a person as if he were at last re-entering the Garden of Eden.

> They were especially experiences which I had had with my parents in the holidays, which I always enjoyed particularly. These images of my past life flitted quickly by me and were grouped in a retrograde order, until they reached the time when I was about five years old. These pictures were filled solely with people who were close to me and whom I loved. So I saw my parents and sisters, but also the friends whose company I enjoyed. They were all purely affirmative, happy and agreeable pictures.[47]

Other people experience dying almost exclusively in the form of extremely intense musical impressions, as if they themselves were the music. We shall come back to this later. But these sensations belong to the subject of the life panorama when it is not merely a fantastic music of the spheres which is involved, but the dying person's favourite music, which he remembers from his lifetime and which he suddenly experiences with a new and hitherto unknown awareness. He wanders through it as if it were the expression of his release from the material world and some harmonious liberation: as if he were hearing it for the very first time, and yet as if it were simultaneously the very symbol of his earthly existence.

It is by no means unusual for the dying person, after the cessation of bodily feeling, to be granted the liberating life panorama as he experiences the resolution of his most immediate conflicts as well. Like the rest of us, my friend H.S. suffered very much during the war from the fact that the post so often needed many weeks before it reached us in the front line. On the very day when his abdomen was torn to pieces, he had told us during the morning how weighed down by worry he was about his father, who was seriously ill, and his brother, of whom no-one knew whether he was dead or a prisoner. We were certain that my friend was dead and covered him with a tarpaulin. But then he woke up again, shortly before he died, and told us with the happiest of faces that he had met them all, his father was digging in the garden among the roses, and his brother was playing in the grass with their little sister and the dog. As he said this the snow fell on his face—the snow under which we were then forced to leave him.

Perhaps H.S. was only able to tell us the beginning of what he underwent in dying, the part which occupied his unconscious the most. We hear again and again that the comforting pictures supplied by the memory lead from the present progressively backwards through the years, right to earliest childhood, as if the dying person in his approach to death now had to accomplish the re-entry into his birth.

Unconscious as I was, I saw, as if it had been in a film, several pictures out of my earlier life, which curiously enough ran backwards from the present to the past. First of all I saw the picture of my mother; she was smiling at me, although at that time she was in hospital with gall-bladder trouble. The certainty of her being restored to health was associated with my mother's picture. As her image faded, my father was standing cheerfully in front of me. He was holding my hand and climbing a hill with me, in the place we came from. There were a lot of flowers right and left of the path. He pointed them out to me. The whole countryside was blooming and bathed in sunlight. I found a big stone and turned it over: it was weightless. On the back of it was a quantity of the most beautiful rock crystals. They were grouped together like a cathedral. I was delighted with them. As we went on, I was suddenly together with a lot of other children in a big flowery meadow. I could hear clear tones, sounding in a gentle rhythm. We danced together. Suddenly my brothers and sisters were round me. When they fell behind, the little girl I was friendly with came towards me. She died when she was six. Now she had light, shining hair. I was just as small as she was and the same age. In the last picture I felt as if I were about three years old. All at once I was lying in my cot. My grandmother's thin, tender face was leaning over me, looking at me kindly. I knew immediately that it was my grandmother, although I had never been able to remember her. She was lit up by a broad sunbeam. At the same time I heard clear tones like a woman's voice. It could have been my mother. She always sang a lot. But now I had regained my senses. I was sad and disappointed that now all these lovely pictures had disappeared.[48]

For us these are naively related stories, but I should hesitate to shrug them off as the reflexes of physical occurrences. We shall discuss this question later. Is the immensely complicated life of the human soul, the treasury of a person's past, to be reduced in its final hour to a tale from a children's story-book? Does it not seem more probable that the dying person becomes childish, like a senile old man, because the switches in his brain are breaking down, rather than that we at long last attain the Gospel's high requirement and blessing, and become like little children—people, that is to say, who take existence as a pure, unearned gift, delighted by its incalculable riches?

Let us come back to this experience once more: the dying do not passively register their life panorama like a film. On the contrary, they work with it, and with the self that is realised in it, and which in these texts is so impotent to express itself when faced by this experience. Here now is an account in which we find united, in a detailed testimony of the work accomplished by the soul in dying, much that we have heard up to now about the exit of the self and the life panorama; it is expressed in a symbolism which is not hard to interpret:

On Saturday afternoon I regained consciousness. I was lying in the isolation hospital and there was a drip attached to my arm. The more awake I became, the clearer my situation was. I had returned to a world which I felt to be small, futile and unreal. I knew that I had been somewhere 'outside', in a state which knew neither space nor time. On the one hand I was happy when I thought about what I had experienced; on the other I was at the same time very disappointed that now I was back again in my shattered body. But what had I actually experienced? It hadn't been a dream. I felt that the whole thing was far too close to reality for that. I had been in a completely different world. One forgets dreams so quickly, and certainly their details. This experience remains clearly before my eyes. I was in some high-up place. It was dark all round me, but in spite of that I felt quite at ease and found my way about quite easily. As I looked round I was able to see that there was quite a high wall in front of me in the darkness. On this side of the wall there was a flight of steps. They kept close to the wall and led onwards to places that got increasingly bright, further away from me, and upwards towards the right. Then the steps disappeared in a strong, clear radiance.

From the place where I was, I could see, not far away from me, a brown, wrinkled, frail little man. He wanted to climb the steps up to the light. But it seemed as if he wasn't moving. I saw as I looked more closely that he was carrying a burden on his back. It looked like a sack, and was evidently so heavy that the man's knees were shaking. I told myself immediately that I must help the poor old fellow, for I felt attached to him and responsible for him. But at the same time I realized that from up here there was little I could do for him.

He hadn't got far along his dark pathway up to the light. Round about him it was black, the path seeming to consist of soft coal dust. It only got lighter further up. I was sorry for the little man. We belonged together. How could we get out of this situation?

Although I was alone with this poor old creature, I felt the presence of someone else: there was a voice inside me which immediately and clearly responded to everything I thought. How shall we get out of here? The voice close by answered: after all, you always wanted to experience and do great things: now is your chance! But I can't, I answered. The voice said: you may leave your body, which is standing down there. The way up is open to you. But isn't it wrong to leave my poor tormented body here, in the middle of the road to the light? You must help him through your will! It's an enticing offer, to leave my body, I said, but I have decided to go on struggling ...

I struggled with myself for a long time. Then I saw the little man again. He had meanwhile progressed a bit. But as I watched him, he again stopped moving. I then discovered that he had grown. And the sack seemed to have become smaller and lighter. The little man now had straight legs and his knees were no longer bent. I was glad that I hadn't left the creature, and turned again to my invisible 'friend'. I think we shall manage it. Your closeness has given me such strength. The voice answered: you see, the will to true and honest struggle always reaches its goal.

The answer was vague, but I was immediately filled with warmth and gratitude. I had encountered my 'friend'. He had given me hope. I shall never forget him. Moreover, from that time on I never felt separated from him. He was at my side. He talked to me out of myself. I saw that the being at my feet was now no longer carrying any burden at all. And then I found myself once again in my own body, here in hospital. Everything seemed to me absurd and pitiful.[49]

The message of the soul's 'leader' does in fact seem not only vague but trivial. It is a cliché: that honest will reaches its goal. Nor is the contradiction solved, that this wisdom is conferred on the self, although the self expressly refuses to follow the 'friend's' advice, that is, did not leave the 'poor tormented body' to itself, in order to press more freely towards the light. I think it is possible that in this inner experience the narrator's self has helped to complete the work which his body was doing at the same time, in expelling the poison with the help of an infusion of new blood, thus being revived. Sympathy with 'the poor creature' and the reducing of his burden could be an expression of the reviving will to return to this body. At the same time this return, even though it is felt as being a wretched one, brings a benefit with it, once it has been completed: the self has not, it is true, arrived at the light 'up there to the right', but, turning in that direction, it has at least been able to experience and observe the identity of 'light' and 'friend'; and it has seen that the little brown man, the sick body, is also freed from the burden of the past and, now upright on the path, has got a little further towards the heights.

But apart from all the possible interpretations, this story confirms that the process of the self's escape in dying can be linked with a working up, a refurbishing of past and present life. Here the life panorama is associated with the experience of an imaginary landscape, with its view of wall, path, and light; it is part of the experience of wandering through some transitional region for which we have a hundred examples in the history of myth. The scene has sombre features. The picture is bare and depressing. The narrator wants to be free, but isn't.

S.v.J., whose 'exit' experience we already know, gives a very different account of his life panorama:

Then a fantastic, four-dimensional drama began, composed of countless pictures and reproducing scenes from my life. At the time I gave 2,000 as the number, for the sake of getting some idea of the magnitude, but it might just as well have been 500 or 10,000 scenes. In the first weeks after the accident I was able to remember 150 to 200. Unfortunately I was not able to record these reminiscences on tape.

But the number is not really important. Every scene was

complete in itself. The 'producer', curiously enough, had put this play together in such a way that I saw the last scene in my life—that is to say, my death on the road near Bellinzona—first; whereas the last scene in the performance was my first experience—my birth. Every scene had a beginning and an end, only the order was reversed. So I began by re-enacting my death. The second scene showed me the journey over the Gotthard, for the first time not as driver but as passenger, in brilliant sunshine, with little snowcaps on the mountains. I was feeling happy.

I saw all the scenes, not only as protagonist but as observer at the same time. It was ... as if I had experienced the whole simultaneously from above and below, or from the side, or alternately from every side. I hovered above myself. I observed myself from every side and listened to what I was saying. My whole soul was a sensitive instrument, my conscience immediately weighed up my actions and judged me and what I did. But curiously enough my evil actions were not included in this drama. I saw only 'scenes' in which I had been happy. Harmony was not only in me myself but also in the whole of the world around, as well as in the souls of all the people involved. It was very curious that these harmonious memories turned up even in the scenes which showed what would be called evil actions, according to our present social morality, or would have been sins, even deadly sins, according to our religious views. . . .[50]

The reporter then claims that he experienced something like a reversal of values in this life panorama. Step by step what was negative had been repressed, whereas he acquired a critical eye for everything in his life which he had not done of his accord, however good it might have been.

We shall have to accept the experience of the life panorama—a curious mode of justification of the self—as part of the experience of dying. An interpretation based on depth psychology would pick up Sigmund Freud's notion of 'censorship'. Freud thought that our subconscious accompanies our life as censor, in the sense that it suppresses our judgements about our wrong actions. Only this 'censorship' makes it possible for us, moreover, to take up our burden again every morning and to begin the day as if we had not always simply failed previously. Freud went on to take numerous examples to support his theory that in our dreams this censorship is certainly relaxed, but not abolished. Even in dreams, the subconscious tries to cast a veil of symbols and images over the oppressive memories we shrink from and the desires that shock us, attempting to prevent truths which might destroy us from coming to life. It needs a particular effort to let our conscience, our knowledge, which pronounces judgement on good and bad actions, speak. The subconscious strives against this effort. In the life panorama experienced by the dying, we might supplement this theory by saying that the subconscious gives up the struggle, as it were. Now, therefore, through the abolition of the court of justice which Freud called censorship, the person is bound to be manifest. What he knows about himself is no longer subject to the life-promoting censorship which has so long forbidden this knowledge to be expressed. Up to now he had very seldom admitted what was good and what was bad about himself. Now it has become possible; his consciousness demands a reckoning.

In his great story *The Death of Ivan Illych*, Leo Tolstoy entered with the visionary imagination of the poet into the fantasies in which a dying man seeks to render an account for his misspent life. The life of the judge and public prosecutor Illych has been told at length previously, without any judgement being passed on him. In his profession Illych knew how to divide his public life strictly from his private one. He always wanted to live pleasantly and comfortably and achieved his aim, even though he was cursed with a vain and quarrelsome wife. But now, in his incurable illness, he recognises that this pleasant life has been very simple and very ordinary, and yet terrible. He, who had condemned so many with such careful observance of the proper forms, is now condemned himself. He lies dying for three days, noisily and painfully; but as the pictures emerge from his past, the hope also emerges that even now he may be able to make amends for everything. An hour before his death 'Ivan Illych fell through and caught sight of the light, and it was revealed to him that though his life had not been what it should have been, this could still be rectified. He asked himself, "What *is* the right thing?" and grew still, listening.' His family gets on his nerves. But had they not suffered even more from him?

And suddenly it grew clear to him that what had been oppressing him and would not leave him was all dropping away at once from two sides, from ten sides, and from all sides. He was sorry for them, he must act so as not to hurt them: release them and free himself from these sufferings. How good and how simple! he thought. And the pain? he asked himself. What has become of it? Where are you, pain?

He turned his attention to it.

'Yes, here it is. Well, what of it? Let the pain be.'

'And death ... where is it?'

He sought his former accustomed fear of death and did not find it. 'Where is it? What death?' There was no fear because there was no death.

In place of death there was light.

'So that's what it is!' he suddenly exclaimed aloud. 'What joy!'

To him all this happened in a single instant, and the meaning of that instant did not change. For those present his agony continued for another two hours. Something rattled in his throat, his emaciated body twitched, then the gasping and rattle became less and less frequent.

'It is finished!' said someone near him.

He heard these words and repeated them in his soul.

'Death is finished,' he said to himself. 'It is no more!'

He drew in a breath, stopped in the midst of a sigh, stretched out, and died.[51]

The Expansion of the Self in Dying

'In place of death there was light,' says *The Death of Ivan Illych*, and we remember the little brown man who worked himself up into the light. 'More light!' Goethe is supposed to have called, as his last words, as if the rising light was already present to him as he died. The life panorama has passed by. The self, which has left its sick, bodily form, has rendered its account; has allowed the guilt and failure of its existence to file past it; and has received anew the good things of its life, the treasures of its existence. In dying, as in living, we shall all experience the cross, in so far as we have ever taken the path towards wholeness, shall 'inevitably encounter whatever has crossed or thwarted us', as the depth psychologist says. But, if we may be allowed to trust our reports, we shall also enter into light.

The impression of light in dying is an age-old human experience which is buried nowadays. The literature of all cultures is full of testimonies to it. In Buddhism this experience has led to subtle liturgical practices at the hour of death. We read in the *Tibetan Book of the Dead*, for example:

> When the expiration hath ceased, the vital-force will have sunk into the nerve-centre of Wisdom and the Knower will be experiencing the Clear Light of the natural condition. Then, the vital-force being thrown backward and flying downwards through the right and left nerves, the Intermediate State momentarily dawns ... The time [ordinarily necessary for this motion of the vital force] is as long as the inspiration is still present, or about the time required for eating a meal ...
>
> Now thou art about to experience [the Clear Light] in its Reality in the *Bardo* state, wherein all things are like the void and cloudless sky, and the naked spotless intellect is like unto a transparent vacuum without circumference or centre. At this moment, know thou thyself; and abide in that state. I, too, at this time, am setting thee face to face. Having read this, repeat it many times in the ear of the person dying, even before the expiration hath ceased, so as to impress it on the mind [of the dying one]. If the expiration is about to cease, turn the dying one over on the right side ... [so that] the vital force will not be able to return from the median-nerve and will be sure to pass out through the Brahmanic aperture ... [At this moment] the first [glimpsing] of the *Bardo* of the Clear Light of Reality ... is experienced by all sentient beings. The interval between the cessation of the expiration and the cessation of the inspiration is the

time during which the vital-force remaineth in the median
nerve. . . .

After the expiration hath completely ceased, press the nerve of
sleep firmly . . . and impress in these words, thus:

Reverend Sir, now that thou art experiencing the Fundamental Clear Light, try to abide in that state which now thou art
. . . experiencing . . . Now thou art experiencing the Radiance
of the Clear Light of Pure Reality. Recognize it . . . Thine own
consciousness, not formed into anything, in reality void, and the
intellect, shining and blissful,—these two,—are inseparable. The
union of them is . . . the state of Perfect Enlightenment.

Thine own consciousness, shining, void, and inseparable from
the Great Body of Radiance, hath no birth nor death and is the
Immutable Light—Buddha Amitābha.[52]

This is not the place to interpret these sayings from what is for us
a very alien cultural context. They serve only as one of countless
examples that substantiate the importance of light in the experience
of dying. The following account, which has just come into my
hands from Holland, is the latest to reach me while I have been
working on the present book. Is it so far removed from that ancient
instance?

I was a ten-year-old girl. In summer my parents liked to go with
me to the swimming pool on the river. The children's pool was
lined with planks. I could easily stand in it, as I played with the
other children. But once I slipped on the slippery floor. I went
down immediately, came up again, lost my balance once more
and went down again, this time completely. I don't know how
long the drowning lasted, but I do know that I was fully conscious. Afterwards I was able to remember that I had passed
some frontier and had entered into a new reality. Light in profu-
sion shone round me. The main colour was red, passing into
yellow and orange. When I say 'shone round me', I can
remember it as being a reality which eluded the mode of our
perception. It was perception, not as an objective registering,
but—to take a German word—a *Wahr-Nehmen*, in the literal

sense, a finding true, a being surrounded by something so loving and tender that even today I can find no words for it. 'I' remained present, completely conscious, and simply put myself, if I may so express it, into this great hand of light ... until my mother drew me up by the hair. It was a long time before I could overcome the disappointment at being again 'this side' of the frontier and at being taken away from that light. I was quite unable to feel grateful to my mother.[53]

According to the criteria of modern medicine, the film producer Victor S. was clinically dead for 23 minutes. He had had a heart attack at the wheel of his car and it was only thanks to a series of fortunate circumstances that he came back to life again. Two specialists in internal medicine, two surgeons, two laboratory assistants, two experts in respiratory therapy, and four nurses finally got his heart going again, with the help of a heart monitor, oxygen, injections, and electric shocks. He remembers the final impression he had while he was dying as follows:

I was moving at high speed towards a net of great luminosity. The strands and knots where the luminous lines intersected were vibrating with tremendous cold energy. The grid appeared as a barrier that I did not want to move through, and for a brief moment my speed appeared to slow down. Then I was in the grid. The instant I made contact with it, the vibrant luminosity increased to a blinding intensity which drained, absorbed and transformed me at the same time. There was no pain. The sensation was neither pleasant nor unpleasant but completely consuming.

The grid was like an energy converter transporting me into formlessness, beyond time and space. Now I was not in a place, nor even in a dimension, but rather in a condition of being.[54]

We shall talk about this 'new state' in the next chapter. Here, first of all, is some further evidence of the 'light' experience met with by the dying. For Elizabeth B. it followed directly on the life panorama and, like the latter, had religious features.

Then came the Light. A brilliant, white Light, blinding in its unearthly radiance.... It suffused my whole being, lifting me to the indescribable height of sublime ecstasy; complete at-one-ment with the Divine Essence, at the all-pervading consciousness of the Cosmic, of God.

Slowly began the return to my body and the world. Gradually I withdrew into my lifeless body. But the light remained, and, intuitively realizing, during this delicate operation, that it was of the utmost importance to retain as much as possible of its radiant life-giving vibrations, I concentrated my whole attention on it.[55]

The experience of light and colour is not infrequently associated with music; we are even told of voices. Mrs F.L. was clinically dead for half an hour. Her heart was got going again by means of an adrenalin injection. When she opened her eyes she said:

I was a long way away. Did you call me back? ... How it actually happened I don't know any more. All at once I heard a fine, high-pitched humming. Or was it the colours round about me which radiated these sounds? I was floating in a long tunnel, which first of all seemed quite narrow and then got wider and wider, wider and wider still the further forward I floated. Above me it was dark red and in front of me a very dark blue which got lighter the higher I looked. I was moving forwards along this tunnel. The weightlessness was wonderful. I heard a voice a long way away. It was no longer the singing and humming of the colours; this voice called my name. I knew the voice, and I know too that I tried to remember whom the voice belonged to. While I was floating through the tunnel I couldn't remember. But I know now. It was the voice of a person who died many years ago and whom I have often thought about. Then I heard footsteps too, as if someone were going through a big tunnel, walking noisily. The footsteps echoed behind me. I hurried forward, for I wanted to find the person who was calling me. I had to look for him somewhere where the dark blue grew towards me out of the opening of this funnel. The humming became higher and more beautiful. The colours too became clearer, seemed to merge into one another in a multicoloured play of a thousand nuances, and then to unfold again like a bunch of flowers. Every colour had a sound. And all these colours and sounds together produced a wonderful music which filled me and drew me forwards.[56]

We shall hear later how this woman was fetched back from this experience, returning to her body. She then lived another twelve hours. After that she died a second time, for ever. Light, colours, and music are the dominating experiences in dying. Compared with these, the experience of the spoken word is of secondary importance. Even in the last account a voice is only mentioned; we are not told what it said. The words were not remembered. And when, in giving an account of the life panorama, the narrator talks about meeting people, usually his nearest and dearest, or when we are told that he carried on conversations, the material we have never tells us what was actually said. In contrast we must point to the other, persistently recurring experience of weightless floating in a space which is not experienced as space at all. 'I drifted in marvellously pervaded interim regions' we heard from Paul Anton Keller.[57] But he was 'scarcely aware', on the one hand, of the dimensions and character of this intermediate kingdom; and yet on the other hand he experienced it 'with much more alert senses than it is given to dreamers and the mentally confused to do'. Yet again, the vision is apparently 'remote' from all the sensory organs.

The experience of peace and happiness was indescribable. Whatever had once bothered me seemed a world away—could not even be recalled in thought. Thought—did I still have the capacity to think? It seemed to me as if everything had dissolved into feeling, into clear perception, which declared itself to me as heightened and transfigured reality. I already knew what it was to faint and to be under an anaesthetic; but the sensory world in which I now found myself was infinitely clearer, remote from all organs and nerves ... Suddenly music began. These sounds didn't in any way resemble music in its earthly definition. Somewhere, above these divine melodies, must be the kingdom of eternal clarity and peace which I was now floating towards with immense longing.[58]

These elements, the feeling of weightless floating, the experience of light and music, can also be associated directly with the life panorama. This light is then poured over the reanimated past. This is how the Swiss geology professor Albert Heim experienced it when he had a fall in the Alps; he gave a lecture (which attracted much attention) on the experiences he had during the few seconds of his fall.

Then I saw, on a far-away stage, my whole life unrolling in front of me, in an immense number of pictures. I saw myself quite objectively; I played the main part. Everything was transfigured and beautified by a heavenly light. I experienced neither fear nor pain. Even the memory of sad events didn't cause me any grief. Beautiful and lofty ideas predominated and linked together the individual scenes; and, surrounded by glorious music, I felt as if I were bathed in heavenly peace. I became more and more enveloped in a magnificent blue sky, with pink clouds and delicate violet shades. In this ideal atmosphere I floated along gently and painlessly.[59]

These dying visions are colour and sound experiences simultaneously—what the psychologist calls synaesthesias. The observer floats freely in an indefinable space, claiming that he perceived the whole scene with extreme clarity. Colours and sounds, light and music, often appear as abstract impressions, but quite frequently they are defined: 'a magnificent blue sky, with pink clouds', or (from the lips of a four-year-old child who was revived after drowning), 'I was playing with angels on a lovely flowery meadow'. Earlier experiences doubtless form the basis of these experiences. But only the basis, the material. What the dying person experiences is not so much this material as its tremendous visionary intensification. Only this intensification of the experience of reality can provide a reason for the euphoric happiness of which the reports continually speak.

The following case comes to us from Russia. It is a detailed account of the happiness experienced in dying. Because of an unhappy love affair, a man had hanged himself on the railings of a building on Red Square in Moscow. The guard cut him down at dawn and told his officer, who phoned Professor Brunchanenko, having heard of his experiments with animals. The man's death had been ascertained hours before, the report tells us; but in his laboratory Professor Brunchanenko connected him to the 'artificial heart' and brought him back to consciousness. Finally the man told in a low voice:

I was in another country, where I had never been before. It was very big and so beautiful that I would like to go back there. I can still taste the water that I drank there. There was a big spring, and I drank from the spring. I saw flowers which were three times as big as our flowers. They smelled as even the most beautiful flowers, at the height of summer, don't do with us. I saw a lot of people a long way away. When I wanted to run towards them, they disappeared as quickly as I ran after them. A drummer stood under a huge tree, which seemed to have grown as high as the sky. This drummer didn't run away from me. Someone told me that now everything was all right and that I could even fly if I wanted to. Then the drummer grew as big as a tree. I couldn't see him any longer. Then I ran further and further through this beautiful green country, calling loudly for someone. I know now that I was looking for my mother. But she has been dead for a long time. I looked for her, and someone told me too that I should soon find her, but that it would take a little while. Then I went to sleep under the big tree that reached up to the sky. And now I don't know: did I dream that life in another country, or am I dreaming a bad dream here and now?' The man lived for another four days. The artificial heart could not keep him alive any longer. Before he died he whispered: 'I am longing for the green country'.[60]

Almost everything in this account can seemingly be interpreted in the light of the dying man's situation. Intense experiences of tastes and smells are apparently often reported by people who have been hanged; the drummer could be explained as the subconsciously witnessed beating of the artificial heart; and the vain search for the mother is explicable as longing for the beloved, for whose sake the man had died. Yet his dying experiences can hardly be fully harmonised with his personal, living ones. The latter cannot explain how death—particularly a death which we associate with the maximum degree of horror and fear—should make an archetypal paradise flower in the depths of the soul: the beautiful green land, with the bubbling springs, the huge flowers, and the tree in the midst growing up to the sky (that is to say, joining heaven and earth), the tree under which it is good to rest. So did Adam rest under the Tree of Life in the Garden of Eden; so did Buddha rest in the lotus under the trees of the land of Amithaba, of whose reality of knowledge and light, in their all-pervading glow, we have already heard at the beginning of the chapter.

In all accounts of 'the final hour' which I have come across, this decisive phase of dying is unanimously described as a state of felicity, a felicity which cannot be formulated in words. The American writer Caresse Crosby was saved from drowning when she was a child, just like our Dutch informant.[61] Even after she was grown up, this was her considered opinion:

> I was aware of the efforts being made by the people who wanted to bring me back to life, but I didn't help them. I was only seven years old, and was a sheltered child, without any worries. In spite of that, no moment of my later life has equalled that one in pure bliss.[62]

The architect S.v.J. found it possible to say something definite about the nature of this bliss; we have already heard about the escape of his self[63] and his life panorama.[64] He goes on:

> I felt that I was floating and at the same time I heard wonderful sounds; and I perceived forms, movements, and colours which fitted these sounds. I felt as if someone were carrying me, calling me, comforting me, higher and higher into the other world into

which I was now permitted to enter as a newcomer. A divine peace and a harmony I had never felt before filled my consciousness. I was utterly happy and wasn't bothered by any questions. I was alone; no earthly being disturbed my calm. The music became louder and louder, and sweeter and sweeter; it flooded everything and was accompanied by ever more beautiful visions. It is really indescribable. It might perhaps be roughly compared with Walt Disney's film *Fantasia*, where Disney tries to reproduce musical impressions in colour, form and movement. The colours that I saw—brilliant, crystal clear, shining, and yet also pastel in hue, I could compare with the ones which I had seen during a sunset on a flight from Geneva to New York. I have looked for those colours ever since that hour when I was dying. I have turned to painting on glass; for the crystal-clear colours of the stained glass, when its facets are flooded with light from various angles, remind me of those marvellously beautiful manifestations of colour.[65]

The Danish clergyman Han Martensen-Larsen has collected a series of accounts according to which the dying experience the peak of their vision at the very moment in which their souls decide in favour of life again. A clergyman was suffering from double pneumonia and his life was despaired of. One night, towards morning, he stretched out in the belief that he was about to die. He had said goodbye to his wife. Then he goes on:

I lay there, fully conscious, and noticed my heartbeat becoming slower and slower; I was just waiting for it to stop altogether. But I also experienced something else at the same time. I was standing on a beach, in the early morning. It was absolutely still; I only faintly heard the splashing of the water on the beach. A thick but shining mist lay over everything, and I waited in intense expectation, for I knew that the mist would soon rise and then I would see Him, there in the light. . . . Then it was as if something inside me had turned over, my heart beat more strongly, and everything had gone. Now coming back to life

seemed agony and disappointment, and this feeling persisted for
many years ...[66]

Auditory phenomena are secondary compared with visual ones
in dying. The operation of the subconscious seems to produce
primarily visual images. Even mixed impressions seem fewer—
colour and music together, the feeling, even the tasting and smel-
ling of a new world, as a remarkable compound of the contents of
the consciousness. I have seldom, however, come across accounts
of words and comprehensible ideas which have been communicated during the act of dying. The reports pass on at most general
statements about voices which the dying person heard as revela-
tions. The following Swedish account is an example:

I came to myself again in the dark, inside a spiral-shaped tunnel.
Far away, at the end of the tunnel, which was very narrow, I saw
a bright light. Then someone began to talk to me. Someone was
there, in the darkness. He began to explain the meaning of my
life to me. I was given answers to all the questions which a
person could ever ask. Now I knew everything, and the knowledge that I had received made me feel indescribably light-
hearted. For it filled me with peace and happiness. The explanation of my life was in my hands: everything was simple, logical
and a matter of course.
    'When you wake up, everything you have heard will be blot-
ted out of your memory', said the voice to me, 'for no-one who
possesses such knowledge can live on earth. But you will be able
to remember that the hard things in your life are now over; you
don't need to be afraid any more. Now go back to your life.'
'No!', I cried, 'I don't want to! Save me from having to go back
there!' 'You must go', said the voice. 'Your time has not yet
come. Now go!'
    Then I became conscious of many voices. I reluctantly opened
my eyes and saw a lot of white coats round my bed. 'I must tell
you something important before I forget!' I cried. 'Oh, she's
waking up. I should never have believed that we could bring her
back to life', I heard someone say, 'but she's still confused'. I

tried to remember what I had been told. But everything had been expunged from my memory ... I only retained the certainty that this life is not the only one, and that one day I shall know that everything has its own meaning and significance.[67]

This account is disappointing in so far as it expressly tells us that the information revealed to the dying person was not verbal information, but was merely a call, in the sense of encouragement; and that she was put off until some future date. At that moment the patient, as she wakes up again, claims to have had 'the explanation of her life' in her possession. Now she no longer knows what it was. 'We cannot describe it in words, it was too beautiful', the dying say again and again about their optical impressions; it was said so 'simply, logically and as a matter of course', we are told in this last account, 'but now all I know is that I knew it once and shall know it again one day'. The dying so often explain that everything they experienced was clear and impressive, supernaturally radiant and comprehensible. But it can only be communicated in rough outline to those who have remained here, simply because the dying person had crossed a threshold. That is why the patient, once he has 'come back', cannot even reproduce them himself. It remains a general impression, coloured according to the circumstances in which the person died and by the temperament of the dying person himself—the impression of another, paradisal world which he has been permitted to enter for a short time.

The following anecdote told about La Boétie, a friend of the philosopher Montaigne, is relevant here:

Towards 4 o'clock in the morning, La Boétie suddenly started up out of sleep. He was heard wheezing 'it is well, it is well, let him come when he will, I am waiting for him quite composedly, quite calmly'. He was talking about death. In the evening, when he was no more than the shadow of a man, he bade that Montaigne be called. 'My friend and brother', he said to him, 'may God so dispose that I experience in reality the scenes that I have just seen!' And since he did not speak again, but struggled painfully for breath (for his tongue began to deny its service), Montaigne put his face close to his and asked, 'What scenes, brother? Do you not wish me too to enjoy them?' 'I do wish it', he answered, 'but brother, I cannot. They are great, wonderful, endless and inexpressible.'[68]

In a contemporary account, the same experience is described as follows:

While I was still consciously thinking about dying, I saw, in this quite conscious state, pictures before me in which all the colours of the rainbow were intermingled. These pictures enraptured me. I felt neither fear nor pain. Everything round me is peaceful. I have a feeling of well-being and joy. Then I feel myself lifted from the earth into the heights, feel myself drifting in space, higher and higher, and see the world spread out at my feet.[69]

The sum of all these impressions of colours, forms, pictures, sounds and voices, which cannot be described in detail, seems to me to lie in the fact that the dying person undergoes a change in himself. The walls of his life, like the walls of his hospital ward, have become transparent. 'The patient's sense of his own individuality', says a doctor about a sick person in a coma, 'and the inner bond with his relatives and all the people he loved when he was alive, remained; but nothing was painful or compelling any more. All the guilt he had felt up to then, all his failures, were experienced as something that had been laid aside. The mood of always belonging to the eternal home and of being himself love, goodness, trust, hope, eternal in character and of the highest degree, determined everything.'[70] The tunnel, about which we have heard so often in these accounts, has been traversed, the dying person has become radiant, together with the light he looks on. It will probably be permissible to interpret this tunnel experience as the change from fear to freedom in dying: salvation peers, and appears, through the suffering.

At the beginning, the self escaped to a place close by, still testifying to its tie with the body; with the life panorama, there was still a compulsion to work over the past; but here, in the stage so frequently described as the ultimate and uttermost happiness, the horizon has widened and the self of the dying person has been raised, in both the literal and the transferred sense, to a weightless floating. It is not only the world that has changed; the dying person himself has been transformed and strives towards new being.

> I found this state very beautiful; it was so divine, so cosmic, so natural. I felt so relieved—indeed liberated, and I felt: at last I have arrived. I thought: I am glad to be dying now. I waited without any fear, but merely with happy curiosity to see what would happen in this dying or death process.[71]

Ultimately the expansion, intensification, and transformation of the person in his experience of dying can only be hinted at in mystical terms:

> This new 'I' was not the I that I knew, but rather a distilled essence of it, yet something vaguely familiar, something I had always known buried under a superstructure of personal fears, hopes, wants and needs. This 'I' was final, unchangeable, indivisible, indestructible pure spirit. While unique and individual as a fingerprint, 'I' was, at the same time, part of some infinite, harmonious and ordered whole. I had been there before.
>
> The condition 'I' was in was pervaded by a sense of great stillness and deep quiet. Yet there was also a sense of something momentous about to be revealed, a further change. But there is nothing further to tell except my sudden return to the operating table.[72]

Eckart Wiesenhütter, a neurology professor who underwent all this personally and was able to assimilate it mentally,[73] thinks that further observation of what happens to the dying will add to our knowledge of these processes. We see that there is a borderline, and ought not to give way to the temptation to leap over death altogether, for example by way of spiritualism. But this final stage of dying already tells us about a transformation of existence. Many of the texts we have read give us the impression that in dying the narrator had already passed through the gateway (which is what we see the end of life as being). Did he already see what lies beyond? Our curiosity would like to be satisfied that he did. But we must be cautious. We want to see, but *what* we shall see—that everyone has to find out for himself one day; it will be his own truth. In the accounts given by people who have come back to life, the very beginning, at most, of the world they cannot on this occasion enter may be visible. That comes out in a story dating from the last century:

> In a little place on the west coast, a young woman was lying in bed. She was going to die. She had tuberculosis and no-one could save her. One day her husband and relatives stood beside her bed, watching her as she wrestled with death. Then they saw her features grow rigid; she turned blue in the face and it seemed as if life had given up the struggle. Her husband, believing that she was already dead, finally could not bear it any longer and shrieked aloud. This cry apparently called life back into the already rigid body, and when the sick woman came to herself, she related that she had had a glorious vision. She had suddenly ceased to know what was going round her, or where she was. She had seen a closed gateway, and an angel in front of it, and the gateway was so splendid that she could not describe it. She had had the feeling that the gateway was going to open; but although she was happy at seeing it, she was none the less frightened at the idea of its opening. Then she suddenly heard her husband's cry, as if from a long way away, and with that the vision disappeared.[74]

The Superconscious Mind, Mysticism, and Drugs

Let me pause there. Many questions arise. But one seems to me of pre-eminent importance. Whatever a person experiences, he experiences in his consciousness. Even what is felt in the act of dying expresses events in the consciousness of the dying person.

We have heard that medicine maintains that dying is the dwindling of the consciousness until its final extinction at the point when the individual dies, this point being ascertainable by the absence of brain currents. The image of the candle suggests itself: when it does not get enough oxygen, its light becomes weaker and weaker, until it finally goes out. But now we have seen that our accounts gainsay this comparison. Dying may often look like that from outside. But we see that from within, viewed in the light of the dying person's own experience, dying cannot be reduced to this simple formula.

The following account, given by a man who had been badly wounded, shows us yet again, with particular clarity, that in dying there is apparently a point at which the plane on which the consciousness operates changes completely. Up to this point the picture of the candle whose light gets fainter and fainter is apt enough; but from this point onwards, the consciousness experiences the entirely different inner world which we have shown in the previous sections: detachment, clarity, peace, expansion, vision, a kind of superconsciousness. I am giving the account without abridgement, so that we can follow the course of events:

I felt a violent blow and fell to the ground. I had been shot in the jaw. No pain, just this blow, so that I see a thousand stars dancing in front of my eyes ... The rest of the night passed in a kind of semi-consciousness. Soon I fainted, then I regained consciousness, then I sank into darkness again ... After I had been put to bed, my first impression was of extreme weakness and tremendous lassitude. I felt completely wide awake, but at the same time I was so weak that I couldn't raise my head from my pillow without feeling that I was going to faint. I lay stretched out at full length on my back, with my eyes open, my body utterly slack and motionless, down to the tips of my toes, in a state of wakeful calm such as I never experienced before and have never known again since. My thoughts were completely clear and unconfused; my brain quite lucid, as if purified of everything that might have clouded it; my memory as alert as if it had just been roused. It was just that I had the impression of being absolutely incapable of expressing any thoughts at all, not in words and not even in gestures.

Physically, I had the impression that some obscure, irremov-

able bodily hindrance or some unbridgeable distance lay between the ideas which were astir in the depths of my self and
their outward realization. It seemed to me that my life was only
hanging by a thread. It seemed to have fled to the foundations,
the foundations of my own self. There it still held its ground, by
concentrating entirely on itself, like a little night-light, which the
least breath of wind from outside could at once extinguish. But
at the same time I felt quite at ease, in a state of calm, relaxed,
withdrawn from myself. I enjoyed this extraordinary inner situation, as I also did the fraternal state of kindness and warmth
which bed means for every wounded soldier—bed after battle,
the dressing station and the ambulance.

I heard the nurse say in a clear voice, 'He has another two
hours'. I can't say that this statement astonished me; I felt much
too weak. But all the same there was still the impact one always
feels when the thing that one had always only viewed as a
hypothesis suddenly becomes a certainty. At that moment I suddenly felt frightened; I became acquainted with violent and tor-
menting inner struggle, the soul's last struggle before the immo-
lation. My consciousness was completely clear while this was
taking place. I shall keep the remembrance of that moment for
ever; pray God it may never disappear from my memory, but
that I can preserve it . . . If life is to be left courageously it must
be lived courageously. We do not take away death's bitterness
by averting our eyes from the inevitable. The first grace was to
have experienced the entry into the tunnel; as second grace I pray
that I may reach the end of it without too much fear. These were
my thoughts . . .

From that moment I felt overcome by utter calm. I knew no
more struggle and no more fear. I was infinitely calm during that
whole night—I might say happy, if this word is given its fullest
meaning.[75]

Widely though these accounts differ from one another, they unite
in saying one thing: the consciousness of the dying person by no
means becomes feebler and feebler, like a dying candle. Nor does it
merely flicker up again, like a candle just before it goes out. On the

contrary, it undergoes an unheard-of intensification, such as it had hardly ever experienced in life.

Here it would seem obvious to compare the changes in the consciousness of the dying with the changes familiar to us from other unusual mental processes. We have already talked about the work of the consciousness in dream[76] and about the visions of the mystics.[77] We might also have drawn on the techniques used to modify the consciousness in the meditative practice of the east, which is at least a thousand years older than Christianity (or five hundred, if we take the canonical formulation of the Bhagavadgita). The self of the perfected yogi steps beside his consciousness, in order to look upon the glory of God and the world as a living whole, a far-flung cohesion, a cosmic harmony quickened and borne up by the one Highest.[78] In the teaching of northern Buddhism about 'the great perpendicular path', the achievement of the yogi's consciousness is expressly compared with its achievement in the act of dying:

> If the disciple can be made to see and to grasp the Truth as soon as the *guru* reveals it, that is to say, if he has the power to die consciously, and at the supreme moment of quitting the body can recognize the Clear Light which will dawn upon him then, and become one with it, all sangsaric bonds of illusion are broken asunder immediately: the Dreamer is awakened into Reality simultaneously with the mighty achievement of recognition.[79]

The mystics have again and again described their experience as a kind of dying. And, conversely, after the accounts of dying that we have looked at here, we shall not hesitate to associate what happens in dying with this mystical experience. It is a matter of man's letting go of himself and entering into a new awareness. To 'give up the ghost' or spirit, as the Bible sometimes calls dying, means giving up the conscious will in order to be capable of receiving the superconsciousness of a new experience. 'Who then holds me back, that I come not to the place where I may so be that I see God and hear him speak?' Jakob Böhme makes the disciple say. 'The master spoke: "Thine own will, thine own hearing and thine own seeing;

and that thou strivest against that from which thou camest. With thine own will dost thou break away from what God wills, and with thine own eyes dost thou see only into thine own will ... so that thou mayst not come to what is beyond nature and the senses." '80

Two other forms of alteration in the consciousness, however, cannot be associated with the experiences of the dying person: decay of the consciousness in the mentally ill and its intensification under the influence of drugs. The child develops its consciousness in a protracted maturing process: first consciousness as the registration of stimuli, and awareness in general, the mental world of sensation; then later, slowly, the consciousness of the self; and finally the consciousness of things and the objective world, and of the super-individual values and laws of existence. In the paranoic, the consciousness degenerates in the reverse order, stage by stage: first the sense of value; then the consciousness of the self, down to animal consciousness. More or less the same may be said of the person suffering from sclerosis and of the prematurely senile. Now, the same has been maintained about the process of dying.[81] But all the accounts known to us expressly contradict this.

It has been observed that the mentally ill regain clarity shortly before death[82] and that the dying are suddenly healed of their neuroses.[83] Medically we cannot say why it is that, although the consciousness of the dying, viewed externally, diminishes step by step, it should in its 'inner life' apparently hurry through the totally different experiences that have been passed on to us. The electro-encephalogram measures the absence of cell activity in the brain, but it can tell us nothing about the mental processes that are going on. Indeed science still does not know today what has to happen for physical changes in the brain also to lead to mental events; and it knows no more about how mental stimuli affect the brain cells. We know the switches between brain and consciousness, body and mind; but we still have no idea how they work. To take a very simple example: we can only say how the outward world impinges on the eye and reaches the optic nerve; how seeing actually happens, we do not know.[84]

If, however, the process of dying is not after all a mental illness in miniature, as it has been said to be, it must surely have some similarity with the alteration of the consciousness in drug addicts? Is the addict not even seeking death, in which he supposes that a final happiness is to be found? Let me name three differences between the consciousness of the drug addict and the consciousness of the dying, according to the accounts we are considering. Firstly, the addict glides out of a waking state into dream, without the exit of the self and the self's accompanying capacity for exact observation of the real physical world which the dying report. Secondly, the drug addict acquires no relationship to his own past as he has truly lived it, such as the dying often experience in the life panorama. Thirdly, it is true that when he is 'high', by yielding up his consciousness of the self, the addict undergoes an expansion of his horizon and a conquest of space and time; and he also has visions of fantastic colours and forms. But these visions are always at the same time visions of suffering. The person is certainly 'expanded' under the influence of the drug, but at the same time he experiences his disintegration and the discontinuity of his sick imaginative world. The feelings of intensification and happiness are usually short-lived and do not have the character of a journey towards bright objectives, about which the dying continually tell us. Ultimately, pictures painted by drug addicts display without exception pre-eminently sadistic features. Beautiful and terrible perceptions are always cheek by jowl or are intermingled. These pictures distort familiar phenomena, seek the garish and the macabre, and generally show that the drug offers happiness as dissolution, if not as horror trip,[85] whereas dying seems to end up in the experience of unity.

Through drugs, healthy young people of today want to visit prematurely the land of the dead, where they have as yet no business to be. What the religious mystics experience as the result of an exertion made here and now, in life, what the sage, in disciplined sublimation, may be able to guess as being the final wisdom, these young people want to snatch at by smuggling a few grams of 'dope' for the 'trip' without any return ticket. But with this they can even ruin their experience of dying, as the following story shows:

Some time ago a twenty-year-old girl was dying of cancer in an

American university hospital. She had guessed the diagnosis weeks before, and was plagued by cramps and shivering fits in her fear of the death that was approaching nearer and nearer. One day she demanded a big dose of LSD instead of the usual medicines. The doctors agreed, as an exceptional measure. A psychotherapist being present, after two hours the drug caused a terrible inward death struggle. The patient experienced her fantasies as an absolute reality. Of her own free will she continually let herself 'fall' psychologically, being, in her unconscious imaginations, tortured and killed, torn to pieces and reduced to a skeleton by piranhas at the bottom of the sea. Afterwards a state of quiet ecstasy supervened and the fear of death gave way to an almost detached expectation. In the short time left to her the patient read accounts of eastern mysticism. The report adds, almost with embarrassment, that she died, smiling and serene.[86]

So ultimately this death on the part of someone who wanted to anticipate dying must be said to confirm my thesis and to fit into our accounts. The dying person's final serenity testifies to the fact that he has relinquished his hold on himself. He has detached himself from what kept him bound to life. We can only express this in paradoxical terms: his consciousness has detached itself from his consciousness in order to reach the new state of super-consciousness, perhaps in conjunction with his unconscious. What we see from outside is that the dying person's body can no longer express itself mentally. We do not know whether he still perceives what is going on round him. He is not asleep, but is apparently not awake either. But as long as his vegetative functions are intact, as long as they regulate his blood pressure, his breathing, his temperature, he also remains accessible for the external world: hardly physically, but mentally; and as long as this is so, he above all continues to possess (as our accounts testify) his living, characteristic inner world, even though we think that he is 'unconscious'.

The statement 'He was fully conscious when he died' is probably almost always incorrect. Forty years ago, in his then popular book *Le Livre de la mort douce*,[87] the Frenchman Georges Barbarin drew on a large number of deaths of every kind, as well as reports by many doctors and nurses, to demonstrate that in all probability there is no such thing and can be no such thing as a completely 'conscious' death. For complete consciousness, to which consciousness of physical sensation must at least belong, is already lost to the patient when the process of dying begins. He no longer 'consciously' feels the physical aspects of dying. But what goes on within him between 'complete consciousness' and 'unconsciousness', that is, the experience of dying itself, seems inexhaustible, although no-one standing round can enter into it, and no instruments can measure it.

The very loss of what we call in everyday life 'complete consciousness' seems to make possible the experience of escape or 'exit', the panorama, and the expansion. That corresponds to the experience of all the mystics: the super-consciousness of the unity of the spirit that hovers protectively round us and receives us can only begin when the soul, in the words of John of the Cross, no longer 'clings to created things' or relies on its own strength out of habit and inclination.

The doctor Sir Auckland Geddee attempted a precise description of the experiences of the consciousness of the dying person in his report to the Royal Medical Society in London. It is the description of his own dying which is given here, although it might have found a place in the chapter on the exit of the self:

On Saturday, November 9th, at a minute to midnight I began to feel very ill, and at two o'clock I finally developed acute gastro-enteritis. I suffered from vomiting and diarrhoea until eight o'clock. At ten o'clock I had all the symptoms of acute poisoning: pulse and respiration were hardly perceptible. I wanted to ring for help, but discovered that I was no longer able to do so, and quite calmly gave up the attempt. I was clear about the fact that I was very ill, and briefly reviewed my financial situation. My consciousness seemed not at all affected, the whole time. But I suddenly noticed that this consciousness was detaching itself from another one, which was also situated inside me. In order to describe it better, let us call it the A and the B consciousness. In everything that follows, my self was bound to the

A consciousness. I noticed that the B personality belonged to my body. As my physical condition continued to deteriorate, and my heart hardly beat at all any more, I realized that the B consciousness belonging to the body was beginning to show signs of a complex make-up, that is to say that it consisted of physical feelings deriving from the head, the heart and the viscera. These components took on independent form and the B consciousness began to crumble, whereas the A consciousness, which was now myself, seemed to be completely outside my body, which I was able to see. I gradually realized that I was not only able to see my body and the bed in which I was lying; I could also see everything in the house and garden; and then I noticed that not only could I see things at home—I could see things in London and Scotland too, wherever my attention was directed. I was told by a source unknown to me, whom I called my mentor, that I was completely free in a temporal dimension of space, in which 'now' was an equivalent, so to speak, of 'here' in the usual three-dimensional space of everyday life. I then saw how the doctor was called and how he gave my lifeless body a camphor injection. I was really annoyed. Then my heart began to beat more strongly, and I was brought back to life. I was very unwilling, because I was so interested and was just beginning to understand what state I was in and what I saw ... I returned reluctantly to my body. And when I was back again, the clarity of the vision immediately disappeared. I had just a glimmer of consciousness still, shot through with pain.

In answer to questions, the informant says of the special character of his new consciousness:

Although I seemed to see with both eyes, I perceived the meaning of things, rather than 'saw' them. I began to see people whom I knew. They seemed to be characterized by the coloured aura surrounding them.[88]

This experience tells us about both a crumbling of the consciousness and its expansion. The consciousness of the personality's iden-

tity with its body dissolves into disparate consciousness centres—
'head, heart, viscera'—in order then, apparently, to disappear completely. The self-consciousness (in the literal sense: consciousness of
the self) detaches itself, becoming, as we have seen in the accounts
of the exit of the self, a new court of appeal. It now observes the
body, with which it had hitherto formed a unity; but then observes
the familiar external world of familiar places in addition, without
apparently having to change its newly acquired detachment. And
the sense of value is experienced by the narrator (as in the story of
the little brown man[89]) as a third voice. This voice, as is usual in
psychology and parapsychology, he attributes to his 'mentor', the
bosom friend and companion, tutor, and steward, with whom the
educated reader is familiar from Homer's *Odyssey*. Here, therefore,
two powers are split off from the self-consciousness: one is a consciousness that sinks downwards, into the body, there apparently
crumbling with the body into the component parts whose unity
had till then formed and guaranteed the 'self' consciousness; the
other a consciousness that speaks from above, as it were, 'from an
unknown source' and gives information about the new present.

Another informant[90] had seen this absence of the consciousness
differently. It seemed to her that the consciousness that had
detached itself from the body was collecting in the head, while she
moved 'upwards'. But at the same time, she no longer felt her body
any more.

But the dying person does not feel this decay of the consciousness
to be something negative, let alone painful. It does not even seem to
him strange. It is true that he always seems to know that this is
something new, but his basic feeling is liberation. Something sinks
down from the self which does not belong to it, and from the self
something rises in the direction of new objectives. In surrendering
his self, the dying person experiences and acquires a light, full of
happiness, that illuminates the world in which he lives.

These changes in the consciousness present themselves in very
varying form. The type of death seems to determine the speed of
the change. It is noticeable, for example, in Professor Albert
Heim's mountaineering experience, from which I have already
quoted,[91] how sharply, when physical consciousness is lost, the

clear vision of a directly impending future can switch over into the
mystical contemplation of the life panorama and the experience of
an expansion, with the paradisal felicity of the spheres. This moun-
taineer had just heard his head and back strike the edge of the rock;
almost at the same time he heard himself falling into the snow at the
bottom of the rocky precipice; and yet, in the seconds between fall
and impact, he had been able to calculate all the possible present and
future consequences of this fall and had, simultaneously, been able
to contemplate the vision of his happiness when liberated from
bodily consciousness.

> If I wanted to tell everything I thought during the few seconds of
> the fall, I would need almost an hour. Thoughts and pictures
> followed one another in a clear sequence. First of all I thought
> over what was possibly destined to happen to me, and said to
> myself: the rock I am being flung over must be a rock face,
> because it's hiding the ground at the bottom from me. Every-
> thing depends on whether there is still snow lying at the bottom
> of it. If there is, there will be a snowdrift underneath, and if I fall
> on it I could escape with my life. If there isn't I shall fall on the
> scree and at this speed I'm bound to be killed. If I'm not dead at
> the end of the fall, I'll take the little bottle of ether that's in my
> pocket and put a few drops on my tongue. If only I don't lose
> my stick; it will be very useful down there. I even thought of
> throwing away my glasses, so that, if they broke, the glass
> splinters couldn't hurt my eyes. But the violence of the falling
> movement robbed me of all power over my hands. Then I
> thought about my friends, and deliberated that when I landed at
> the bottom, whether I was hurt or not, I would call out 'un-
> hurt!', with all my might, so as to relieve their minds. And I also
> thought that I would certainly not be able to hold my geology
> lecture, which was supposed to take place in five days.[92]

This feverish activity of the everyday consciousness in its state of
super-tension and awareness then becomes intermingled with the
euphoric visions of happiness, remote from reality, which we
already quoted. The possibility of an abrupt reversal of feeling

seems to suggest itself. And yet the dying cannot and will not say that the consciousness of the thinking and observing self loses clarity in the very least through this entry into the new medium and the new world. Afterwards, if they are saved, they cannot be sufficiently surprised at the way this change of consciousness came about and at the way they achieved this clarity of vision.

> Later, feeling and thinking my way back into the experience, I discovered why I could not make it a simple recital of events: when I left my body I also left all sensory human tools behind with which we perceive the world we take to be real. But I found that I now *knew* certain things about my place in our world and my relationship to that other reality. . . . These experiences did not 'happen' as if I were on some sort of voyage I could recollect. Rather, I discovered them afterwards, rooted in my consciousness as a kind of unquestionable knowing. Being of a sceptical turn of mind, I am willing to grant the possibility that this is a leftover of some subtle form of brain damage.[93]

The Return of the Self

These accounts come from people who were in a state of coma but did not die after all. Their stories take us a little nearer to death. But the narrators 'came back again' only to be forced later to take the journey into death once more, the journey which we shall all one day have to take for ever. The account of this final return casts further light on their experiences.

The public witnesses world-wide attempts on the part of doctors to wring hours, days, months, perhaps even a few years from death, whenever it is all possible: wherever the technical means are available and the financial ones can be raised. People follow the attempts made to prolong life at all costs with all the interest they bring to a thriller. The story of the Soviet Russian Nobel Prize winner Lev Davidovich Landau became an international subject of conversation and was a best-seller under the significant title, *The Man They Wouldn't Let Die*.[94] Landau lay 'unconscious' for three months with countless broken bones and internal injuries, while a team of more than a hundred first-class doctors kept 'the spark of life' in his body, as was said. They opened his cranium, massaged his heart, filled him with new blood, injected him with costly drugs, until he opened his eyes again. His case was a triumph for the whole of medicine, a milestone in the work of its pioneers, and a model for future techniques in the prolongation of life.

But it is precisely the last chapter in this case that is the saddening one. Professor Landau returned from the darkness of death, but to what? It was triumphantly claimed that he had completely regained consciousness. But it was the consciousness of a sick, tired, sad man, who was never again free of mysterious pains. He was never again as fully aware as he had once been. A glance at his face tells us how frightful the return must be, all the more frightful, probably, the longer it takes and the further towards death a person has been.

I do not know whether Professor Landau said anything about dying and the wearisome journey back. Other people have done so. These experiences may differ widely from one another, but what is said about the return, the re-entry of the self into the body, is practically always the same. The dying person finds the doctors' attempts to bring him back to life painful. He often feels that he is being forced through a bottleneck. He wants to resist; he is sad.

Dr. W.'s account, from which I have already quoted,[95] ends: 'While I stood outside, in the middle of the room, I knew with the most acute feeling of pain that I was in my body again.' Another says: 'I returned to my body reluctantly, and when I was back again, the clarity of my vision of everything disappeared suddenly and I only retained a glimmer of consciousness, shot through with pain.'[96] The writer Paul Anton Keller, who had been knocked down by the maypole, ends his account as follows:

The light that was about to open to me grew dim. I felt as if some loveless force was tearing my self into the depths where I knew my body was, the body which I remembered with aversion. Somewhere I felt pain. Yes, there was no doubt, I was sinking, was being pulled and couldn't ward off the invisible suction, even though everything in me fought against it. Again a wave of the most violent pain shot through me. I was torn out of the broad path of flooding light as if by a brutal fist, and suddenly it seemed to me as if I smelled medicines, tobacco, grass and animals—and there were people too ... And so, from an irrevocably sinking level of gnawing pain, the light of day broke in under my eyelids, a pitiful brightness compared with the world of light I now knew about. The doctor's brow, with its surrounding bushels of hair, appeared, bent deeply over me. Now he raised his head and said to the people standing round, in a voice that seemed strange to me: 'He's alive!'[97]

The patient has to retrace his path. He has first experienced the happiness of getting out, liberation, light, and joy, but now everything is taken from him, bit by bit. This second experience supports the first one:

'Suddenly I felt someone reaching out to me. I couldn't move forwards any more. My feet were glued to the ground. I tried to overpower this hand that was gripping me from behind. I was in pain, while the hand closed round me, tighter and tighter, and the colours in front of me got darker. Finally they faded and ceased to give out sounds altogether. I had worked myself out of the narrow confines of the tunnel towards the wide exit; but now it narrowed round me again; it became so narrow that all at once I was frightened. The hand drew me back, further and further, into a deep darkness that first seemed to be dark red but then turned black, insubstantially black as only eternal night can be. And then I was here. I heard you speaking and experienced a feeling of emptiness and sadness. But you won't understand all that!' [And the sick woman, the account goes on, closed her eyes and wept.] 'Am I very ill?' she asked after a while. 'Do I have to stay here?' The doctor wanted to soothe her and answered that she had fainted. 'That wasn't a faint', she said. 'It was much more than that. I was on the other side. Quite definitely. And please don't go to any trouble on my account. Can't you understand that I am in a hurry to get back to the place which the hand pulled me back from?' Mrs Leslie lived for another twelve hours and then died a second time, this time for ever.[98]

The people involved feel pain because the vision of light disappears again, because the colours are withdrawn and the feeling of harmony is destroyed. One woman, who was brought back to life out of a diabetic coma, put it in quite different words, no doubt stylised through distance:

> I saw that I was being carried away in a quantity of little bits. All the bits were of different colours. Everything has been separated from my trunk, my body: there is the liver, shimmering, a reddish brown colour; there is the heart, with its blood-red funnel, and the lungs. They present a kaleidoscope of colour, deep and beautiful. And I saw how I was led away to the kingdom of light. And I saw the light, much stronger than our sun, which irradiated me. I couldn't bear this radiance—I fell, fell into the darkness again. My body lay broken and scattered. I saw myself looking for the internal organs belonging to it. And I wanted to put them back in their original place in creation. Then I saw the pillars of my backbone, its nerves, with their fine network and ramifications; I saw how the organs in their disintegration looked for themselves again. And I became a life once more, a branch on a living tree.[99]

Pain and care had ceased; now they made themselves felt again, as belonging to this life. The sick person had been raised, he had felt himself borne up, he had floated weightlessly in the light which overwhelmed him; now he has to return again, he is sucked down, drawn, pressed, once more he experiences night, the black tunnel, and then what we call waking up: the brutal everyday present which now seems to him like a dream. If he stays alive, having once been so far away, he experiences life, not with gratitude, as one might perhaps think, but with grief. He seems to himself like someone who has been banished. Perhaps those 'mysterious pains' which Lev Landau suffered from for the rest of his life (in spite of all the injections which he was given almost every day) were simply this pain of return. Eckart Wiesenhütter tells that for years he could not get rid of this 'homesickness for the beyond', the beyond that he had experienced in dying. In retrospect, this is the first and

strongest impression as a rule: the fact that it was so painful to enter
the broad daylight of this world again.

> For myself, what I definitely experienced was the inexpressible
> torment of being torn away from liberation—of sinking back
> into it—of having to leave it again—like a ball, without any
> possibility of volition or resistance. In these initial stages I cannot
> remember perceiving and assimilating anything definite about
> the external world or other people. I—if I was an 'I' at all—was
> in what seemed to be a different, disrupted world—in myself or
> beyond myself.[100]

We heard what difficulties the medieval visionary had in returning. A daemon—in the end a good daemon—tries to prevent him
from entering the earthly world again.[101] Apparently the same
thing happens to the dying person whom we bring back to
life.'Coming back to life seemed torment and disappointment, and
this feeling continued for many years', the tubercular clergyman in
Martensen-Larsen's book tells us, and he[102] goes on:

> Yes, I never really got over it; I was never again able to feel at
> home in the world as I did before. For me this experience means
> that I know ... and I am often homesick for that morning when
> the mist will lift and I shall see Him [Jesus] face to face.[103]

Eckart Wiesenhütter has described in detail the many phases in
which the sick person who has regained consciousness comes to
terms with his experience of dying and reluctantly adapts himself
once more, bit by bit.

> The first thing that I sensed coming towards me from the out-
> side world was hands. It may be that I was still too weak to be
> able to see anything and to recognise to whom the hands
> belonged. But I felt hands, being touched, being lifted, being
> carried or being turned over. Each time when my senses slipped
> away from me again it was again hands that came towards me
> first of all ...

'Painfully and increasingly consciously' the author feels that his 'climbing up from the (non-) depths has probably something to do with rebirth'. Like a little child, he has to grow out of 'the shell of the body' into 'the shell where he is dependent on touch', in order to reach the 'seeing shell' or stage. His relationships to people developed in a new way: he judged them differently from before, more from the instinctive or emotional level; and he became shy of people if he did not have the soothing feeling that they were 'true' friends.

But above all, a longing for death wells up from the subconscious of the person who has gone through the experience of dying.

> 'The being able to die continually dogs me like a shadow', as 'the desire and the longing for release', 'the feeling, which I cannot brush aside, that I shall never again find home and security here, that I can never again here feel quite secure ... '[104]

Seen in this light, the longing for death of the 'returned' is rather a longing for that deep security, the being borne up, and the liberty in light which the dying person has experienced in that multifarious state which I have called the expansion of the self. Another put this melancholy into simple words:

> I know, however, that since my return from that other condition, many of my attitudes towards our world have changed and continue to change. A recurrent nostalgia remains for that other reality. The memory softens the old drives for possession, approval and success.
>
> I ... have just returned from a pleasant, slow, mile-and-a-half jog. I am sitting in our garden. Overhead a tree moves gently in a mild, southerly breeze. Two small children, holding hands, walk down the street absorbed in their own world. I am glad I am here. But I know that this marvellous place of sun and wind, flowers, children and lovers, this place of evil, pain and ugliness, is only one of the many realities through which I must travel to distant and unknown destinations.[105]

This brings us to the conclusions which emerge for our own lives from the knowledge that we have acquired up to now. But before we turn to this subject, we must also attempt to make knowledge yield insight. We have viewed dying from outside; and we have directed our attention to accounts showing what it evidently looks like from within, from the point of view of the dying person himself. How can we bring the two things together? How can we reconcile these experiences with what philosophy, what religion, what the Christian faith all have to say about dying and death?

4. THE INTERPRETATION OF DYING AS EXPERIENCE

Its Speechlessness

We are bound to allow the validity of what we have heard. Our informants have the advantage of us: their narratives agree in too many points for us to be able to carp at them. This is what dying will probably be like for us one day—that is to say, quite different from what we had always thought. Perhaps we ought to have looked about us more carefully: if dying is today what it is described as being, it must surely always have been like that; and then there must have been accounts of it here and there, even if not such frequent ones as in our own times, with their superior medical equipment.

The Tibetan *Book of the Dead*, from which I have already quoted and which was written in the eighth century A.D., has already expressed everything said here. It even maintains that everyone knows in himself that dying is just what we have heard that it is. For, it claims, we have already experienced death at least once: our birth, which our daytime consciousness does not remember, shows us the inner side of the door whose outward side leads out to our deaths. Why did we scare ourselves? For the prospect is so bright:

> On the following Sunday, November 7th, he, Jakob Böhme, departed this life. Beforehand, he called his son Tobias and asked him whether he too could hear sweet music. On hearing the answer 'no', he bade that the doors be opened, that the song might the better be heard. 'And now I go hence into Paradise.'[106]

There is no-one, however, who has told what he had to tell of his own accord, without a reluctance that could hardly be overcome. The experience of dying cuts the patient off from everyone else. Hospital chaplains report that in most cases weeks had to pass before these people could resolve to pass on a single word about what they had been through. Eckart Wiesenhütter has described his difficulties: someone who has returned from the world of the dying is so moved and so enchanted by the 'totally other' which he has encountered 'out there' that to talk about it at all seems to be sacrilege. Mustn't we too exercise a certain respect and observe the limits of the discussion?

I think we are doing this when, summing up, we now try to interpret what the experiences of the dying tell us. For we are doing this because a different kind of dying could help us to a different kind of living. It is impossible for too many people in our time to experience what we are concerned with here. But the interpretation is a translation. We have to reduce to a definition what is told us in images.

For the first thing to notice is this: the experience of dying presents itself pre-eminently as picture experience, as vision. We have seen that all the senses are involved, including—and above all—the hearing. But first, and to a great extent almost exclusively, it is a matter of visions. This peculiarity gives me pause, first of all. We are sceptical about visions in the world of Christian thought. Protestantism as a whole, with its enmity towards images, has banned visions and the visionary from the Church completely. The apostle Paul, an ecstatic of the first order, who apparently experienced the exit of the self and 'translation' in a kind of mystical double life,

being a Jew first of all sought the Word in the other world of his
soul: 'this man was caught up into Paradise . . . and he heard things
that cannot be told' (2 Cor. 12. 3–4). If I were asked what I should
one day like to have in front of me when I die, I should answer with
the epitaph that Sören Kierkegaard had put on his grave:

A little space
    and it is won,
the whole dispute
    to nothing run;
in rooms of roses,
    no joy unspoken,
with Jesus hold
    converse unbroken.

'Converse' as the give and take of soul and spirit, as the exchange
of myself with God and everything he gives me—this would surely
be for me eternity as the fulfilment of my existence. That is why it
troubles me to find speechlessness in the first instance in the experiences of the dying. They say that they are unable to talk about it. 'I
was already in paradise, why do you fetch me back?'[107] they say,
not understanding that they have something important to say to
those others of us who were not 'out there'. And they seem to have
undergone a great deal 'on the other side'. Some of them have
apparently heard voices as well; but they have seemingly not yet
entered into the converse which for me would be important. They
received the vision of paradisal coherences and their selves were led
into inconceivable space, but the interpenetration of nature and
spirit, existence and words, which is so painfully lacking to us in
our present world, is not yet accomplished on this final stage of the
path leading to death. What did they hear? 'A fine, high humming'
and Jakob Böhme's 'singing'. They saw music which was like colours, and heard colours which were like music. Steps 'echoed
behind them' and 'beautiful, elevating thoughts were dominant'. 'I
had the feeling that someone was carrying me, calling me and
comforting me.' But the content of the elevating thoughts, the
calling, and the comforting cannot, apparently, be reproduced by

the dying. They are speechless in the face of what they have been through, and what is to be found in the way of language in their accounts does not possess the depth that I expect. Is the speech, the converse, still ahead? Is it only carried on beyond the threshold towards which dying strives? The hope remains. Knowledge about the way in which I (when once I myself am the knower) shall converse with the Redeemer in 'rooms of roses' has not yet been granted to me through the experiences of the dying who have returned.

This question touches on important connected problems. We must pick these up again when we discuss what comes 'after' death. For that decides whether, as an individual, I shall attain 'eternal life' or 'resurrection', as the Christian faith holds. My self is only an individual as a speaking and hearing subject, as the being who is called by God and who is responsible for himself. If this relation were to be dissolved in the act of dying, then my death would be for ever.

I interpret the speechlessness we find in the case of the dying in the following way. Dying only paves the way for what I am to experience later; the impressions which have been communicated to us are provisional in kind. The 'superconsciousness' of the dying person traverses a zone that is silently overwhelming. He encounters his self anew, torn into a reality which he can at most stammeringly describe. But the gateway to new life has not yet been pushed open. What we are able to know about dying does not free us from the task of believing that our new life—which can only be speech—is the realisation of fellowship with God.

The Will, the Pain, and the Fear

If I set aside this difficulty for the moment, then I draw as a second conclusion from our reports that in dying I must again yield up the will that I so long claimed as my own property. I have already made repeated attempts of this kind during my lifetime. I have discovered, late on and laboriously and with much pain, that happiness or heaven or whatever we call this ultimate treasure and goal simply consists of surrendering and yielding up our own wills. I

give my power impotently away and am in return rewarded with
new clarity of vision and with the superconsciousness of being led
and borne up.

I must leave behind me what I have become accustomed to and
have acquired. To put it in Christian terms: this is the unique
property of the creator and it is therefore good that it should strive
to belong to its creator. In my lifetime I have made repeated new
attempts, and every time it seemed to be a bitter affair, and yet the
only thing that brought happiness: to be there for the God whom I
find in the other person.

And now, thirdly, it emerges (or so I read these accounts) that in
dying, where it is fully accomplished, the whole thing is not bitter
at all. The dying have distinctly told us that pain for them had
ceased to exist as long as they were outside the body. In life, it
seems to me, healing is so difficult because we do not want to lay
down our weapons. Much worse than all the physical pains, for
which we have our nostrums, are the mental and spiritual ones
which we men and women ceaselessly impose on one another—
indeed no doubt have to impose on one another, for the simple
reason that we are spiritual beings with a will that is not always
good; that is to say, does not always want what is helpful for our
fellow men. But our accounts make it seem probable that, contrary
to all the gloomy, horrific images of dying which our subconscious
carries round with it as the heritage of centuries, the final hour
brings liberation from the pain which we have suffered in life.

First of all, with regard to the physical pain which reaches us
through our nerves in the form of sensory impressions: quite apart
from the accounts we are considering, we have numerous testimonies telling us that this disappears when people are dying. It is a
preconceived notion that dying is physically painful. Barbarin
observed numerous deaths and modes of death. He came to the
conclusion that—except in the single case of suicide—dying and
physical suffering are mutually exclusive.[108] Even when the dying
person presents a terrible picture to those round him and seems to
be fighting a final battle for his naked life, with all kinds of move-
ments horrifying to us, so that we talk about a hard or even a
horrible death, he does not, in actual fact, suffer. For his perception

of these processes in his body is reduced to zero, his senses are dulled, his consciousness, as we have seen, is lingering somewhere quite different. To plunge into the region where dying takes place means expressly to escape from physical torment. If the largest part of people's fear of dying and fear of death consists in their fear of physical anguish, we can relieve their minds. We have to endure much more pain in our lifetimes than we have to do when we die. Enquiries from doctors and nurses have elicited material which can be unanimously interpreted. In Julius Bahle I find an account of the experiences of eye witnesses of 4,200 deaths. A 'death struggle' was only observed in 8 cases, but in these the informants could not decide whether the dying person retained such a powerful 'self' consciousness that he would have been able to feel pain. In all the other cases, i.e., 99.5%, an apparently painless death, without fear and without the notorious death struggle, was observed.[109]

Almost all our accounts have shown that dying also confers what are actually beautiful, liberating, and encouraging experiences. It emerges that dying not only leaves physical pain behind; it also frees a person from the much worse mental torment which life has imposed on him, because he was unable to surrender himself to the charge laid on him as human being. The transfiguration which appears on the features of most of the dead, especially when their bodies have resisted and rebelled beforehand, is an indication of this fact that we can hardly overlook.

Something remains on this side of death which looks like what in life we called our body. But it is only our body in form. Medicine and psychology only recognize the body when it is animated body—body informed with soul. The material which remains behind after death is something different, a third thing which we do not need to consider here. From the reports about the exit and the return of the self, however, we know one thing: there is only pain in connection with the consciousness and *through* the connection between the consciousness which escapes and the being which remains behind; or, to put it in the old pictorial language, only through the bond between body and soul. So dying can be equated with entry into the kingdom in which we can suffer no pain, because the organ through which the soul can experience pain has remained behind.

Where someone fights a physical and mental battle against death, where death, as we like to think, fights the deadly battle within us, this happens before we die. What we see is only a reflex, like the reflex shown by the galvanised limbs of a dead frog. The person is no longer here. Earlier, on the first realisation of the fact that he was going to die (which had perhaps long been kept a secret from him), when the doctor declared him to be a 'terminal patient', when all the people in the hospital began to treat him as someone who was now definitely dying, the patient probably rebelled. But then dying began, and he surrendered his will, his willingness, to it. Dying, free from pain and sorrow and therefore free from struggle and tension, can only begin when we have given our consent. Dying is the exit from all struggle and pain, the receiving of pure creatureliness, the creatureliness of Adam, which is capable of yielding itself up, because the yielding is no longer demanded as something that has to be achieved but is achieved as being.

In the penultimate chapter of the Bible, the new heaven and the new earth are described as the era when there shall be no more physical pain, no more mental suffering, and no more 'crying' to frighten us. I read our accounts of dying, fourthly, as the experience of freedom from fear which awaits us. These accounts tell us that the self comes out of the tunnel with its dark confines; it feels itself hovering, held, borne up, and filled with happiness.

We were afraid of dying, but in dying itself we are apparently debarred from fear. Fear, as Martin Heidegger wrote fifty years ago, may be the *Befindlichkeit*, the state of mind, of the finite person who always sees his existence as an individual threatened. But our accounts suggest in their peculiar speechlessness, by means of all kinds of symbols, that the dying person no longer finds isolation and threat to be the ground of his existence:

I saw pictures before me in which all the colours of the rainbow were intermingled. I felt neither fear nor pain. Everything round me is peaceful. I have a feeling of well-being and joy. Then I feel myself lifted from the earth into the heights, feel myself drifting in space. . . .[110]

If comparisons have any meaning here, I think that the metaphor of the lock on a river is an apt one. When dying begins, we seemingly remain in the water of the river which we know. The body is lying in bed, and its spirit still animates it. But a gate has been closed behind it, shutting out the flow of the old, black water. The person has consented to the transition, and slowly, before the other floodgate can be opened, different water flows in, carrying him higher and higher, so that he can reach the level on which he is now to float when he presses out of the tunnel and the black water of his fears into the light, this new thing. 'In the world you have tribulation', says our Bible (John 16.33); 'In the world you are afraid', says the Luther version. But the world is to be overcome. The belief that this happens through Christ fits in here without difficulty, for it is Christ who goes ahead, into the dying and into the death of all those who with him have to die. As their future, he is also their present.

In our accounts the dimension of the future seems to be strangely suspended in the present of the experience. And just as the dying person no longer suffers pain, because he has left the organ of pain behind him, in the same way he can no longer experience fear, because he no longer has to take care of the future. For fear is, after all, our awareness that something dreadful is about to happen. When it has happened, fear is a thing of the past as well.

Body and Soul
We must spend a little more time on the fifth and last point that particularly concerns me about these accounts. Whereas up to now we were dealing with purely negative things—with corrections to our previous view of dying—we now, after that, ask to what extent new being and new knowledge are signalised in these experiences. The mysterious cessation of speech, that disturbing phenomenon which was my starting point, could perhaps find its explanation in what we now have to discuss.

Most of our accounts talk freely about the fact that dying prepares the severance between body and mind, or soul, which is then completed in death. I have done the same in the present chapter. It has been the customary idea and the customary way of speaking since the days of the ancient Egyptians and Greeks. And all the experiences which the dying pass on to us seem to confirm this severance: the self leaves the body, sees the body lying beneath it like an empty shell or a discarded dress. The self, the soul, then assumes a life which no longer requires the body. It sees its past life repeated and observes it, free from the body. At the same time, however, it views the past more clearly than before, and like a judge who has no personal interest in the accused. The soul finally rises far beyond the body and has visions and 'auditions' which it knew nothing of as long as it was in that body. The self—we usually call it the mind or soul—now seems free to enter on a new flight. It knows nothing of the presence of the body, and therefore knows no pain; it is not aware that its life has any future, and it therefore knows no fear; the past seems transfigured, and consequently guilt bears a different aspect.

But just as our usual talk about consciousness proved to be too superficial, so at this point I have difficulty too. Can a person be so simply split up into body and mind, as if he consisted of two halves? We think we know what dimensions we are talking about, yet with all our talk we are only pushing deeper into further mysteries. Science neither knows what the body is, nor what the mind is. If it pretends to know, it is pursuing mythology. Monistic attempts at an explanation have proved misleading. Materialism has long since ceased to be scientifically substantiable. The mind or soul is not merely the physical life's experience of itself, the external world in its inner aspect, as Novalis held. But the body is not only the instrument of the soul either; nor is it merely the soul's appearance, as spiritualists ever since Aristotle have believed (both theories making it possible to explain everything as deriving from a single principle). We like to maintain the existence of this scale, but up to now no theory has explained how organic life (and, deriving from it, the spiritual and mental life) arises from inorganic. Medicine says that body and mind are 'inwardly connected yet divisible substances' and admits that attempts to localise the mind in the body have failed. We see increasingly clearly how close the connection is between physical and mental processes in people, and that human life can consequently only be conceived of as a totality and unity of what are still the pre-scientific dimensions of body and mind, or soul.

This gives rise to difficulties in understanding the experiences of the dying that have been passed on to us. Science, like the rest of us, knows all about the mental and spiritual realities which go far beyond the physical ones. To that extent it talks about the mind as a 'separate' substance. But on the other hand it only recognises the mind in its 'joint functioning' with the body; as if without the body there would be no mind. The two are connected and yet not one, open to separate observation and yet closely related to one another. The image of the body as the garment of the soul goes back to Plato. He also talked about the body as the prison of the soul, or thought of it as the shell and the soul as the oyster: the two-fold division is rigorously carried through. These images contradict the insights of contemporary psychology, and we cannot conceive of the relationship between body and soul in such external terms. The garment is something secondary, distinct from the body; it clothes it, warms it, and adorns it. But it has no relationship to the body which helps to determine the latter. The Bible never thinks in such simple categories. It knows that man does not *have* a body and a soul; he *is* body and soul.

I could rediscover in another image what the experiences of the dying suggest and what modern science has found out and what the Christian faith can assume: the image of the organ and the musician. But what we understand by life is not the organ (the body) on the one hand and the musician (the mind or soul) on the other; life is the music itself. Human life would be the manifestation of this co-operation of two separate and at the same time functionally united substances, the music that we hear. When the player gets up, life is really and radically at an end (for death can only be thought of in radical terms); and we see no more than the dead organ, which can no longer sound of itself. What we could hear—what life gave us as the unity of body and soul and the fruit of their co-operation—is past and gone. When I am dying I may just still be able to see that the player is standing up. He goes out. Where to? Can he exist without this instrument? Apparently. But who or what will he be?

I have gathered together the varying experiences which occur at the height of the act of dying under the heading 'the expansion of the self', and we have considered what may go on in the dying person's consciousness. Consciousness, the self, the soul are names for different aspects of the one thing which we circle round for so long and yet cannot grasp exactly. The self or the soul (or so it seemed to us after these narratives) swims out, as it were, even before death, separated from its body, towards a glorious experience. Together with everything that is to be 'seen' and 'heard' there, it is an experience of liberation, of resolution, of expansion of the self's own dimensions and its own depths. The self, we have already heard, does not disappear as it does in the case of drug addicts and the mentally ill; on the contrary, it acquires something like a superconsciousness, a new dimension. But it is a dimension of its own self. It has its own identity. We notice, however, in most of these accounts that this identity does not encounter other identities in that new space—identities such as make up our life here and that produce fellowship, converse, and conflict between different people. We heard about voices and about beings who, protecting and accompanying, approach in great numbers;[111] the mystic in his death-like 'translation' meets angels and daemons.[112] In these images the consciousness formulates incorporation in a different, larger, and brighter spiritual world.

The dying person, at all events, finds that he is growing beyond the organic and mental categories, in which our individuality expresses itself, into a higher form; and yet he remains conscious of still surviving as a person—the person belonging to the soul which bears his name. He lets go, without himself being let go of; he achieves surrender without being lost; he is resolved but not dissolved; he thinks that he belongs to a greater whole without thereby being himself any less, as one might suppose. In a television discussion on this subject, in which I took part, a Swedish doctor said: 'As long as we are this side of dying our self is like a grain of salt. The moment we step over to the other side, we find that the salt falls into the water: its external form and concentration disappears, but the water becomes salty.'[113] This illustration seems an apt one. But it does not capture what the Christian thinks.

Since today we scientifically recognise a person's body only as an animated body and a person's mind only as the body's animation, we are not capable of saying what the separation of mind and body is. Probably what is separated is inadequately described by the word 'soul' or 'mind'. One of our informants talked about the self of the dying person which is more than a self—it is the distilled essence of the self.[114] Science only sees the earthly person correctly when it sees him as a totality. Yet dying is something like a separation, but apparently not in a negative sense: we lack the proper word for it. For in our accounts this separation seems like a homecoming and as the purest felicity, as a transition to a new being similar to what takes place at our birth. None of our informants has given us the impression that anything was given up. We talk about 'departing this life', but the departure is as much a going forward, a going on in dying. What goes on? Every one of the dying we have met in this book gives his account in full consciousness of his own indestructibility.

It also makes us think, and is equally incompatible with what science tells us today, that the accounts testify, without any attempt at explanation, that though the dying person was no longer bound to what we call 'matter', he still perceived his immediate surroundings by means of a sensory apparatus, and later his more remote—indeed very far off—surroundings too. And he perceived them, as was continually stated, in the literal sense. Is it not one of the oldest premises of thinking man that like can only be known by like? Yet here 'matter' is supposed to have been observed from outside matter; here senses are supposed to have performed their function without the sensory organs. But this too could be an artificial confrontation of opposites, since we do not know what 'matter' really is.

I have drawn attention to the extra-physical mystical vision to which there have been witnesses at all periods. It may offer a comparison to what happens in dying. The grain of salt does not only dissolve in the sea because the condition of the aggregate has to be altered. The dying person does not merely partake of a super-individuality. His individual self is preserved in the medium of the general, and the new being, as the apostle Paul testifies (1 Cor. 13.12), is pre-eminently the new level of knowledge. What the dying with their faltering texts tell us about their greater clarity and what approaches complete knowledge belongs within this context.

These are all contradictions in the world of our logic. The dissolving of the grain of salt in the sea is supposed not to be its destruction, even though the grain no longer exists as far as we can see. The individual is supposed to be absorbed into super-individuality, yet without perishing, so that the Christian belief in the re-creation of every individual seems not untenable. Our accounts do not set up dogmas, nor can they be set up. For our dogmas do not stand the test of reality. They are indications and attempts at putting into words what cannot be grasped in words at all, attempts, that is, at substituting one image for another. We must be quite clear about the fact that everything which we can say here from our present level of knowledge about the other images is at most an approximation.

This applies without any doubt to the dying themselves who have given us their reports. One of them can only make clear to himself what he experienced in the categories of eastern philosophy:

> One of the greatest recognitions granted to me during death and after many hours of meditation is the principle of vibration ... For me, since that time 'God' has come to represent a source of primal energy, inexhaustible and timeless, continually radiating energy, absorbing energy too, vibrating constantly ... it is perfect harmony ... Different worlds are formed from different vibrations, the differences being determined by the frequencies ... Consequently different worlds can exist at the same time and at the same place, since the vibrations that do not correspond have no influence on one another. They are there, but not there for us, just as radio waves or electro-magnetic energies permeate nature without doing any damage. Suitable

instruments are necessary to measure them . . . In the same way psychic and pneumatic energies are conceivable as vibrations and independent worlds, and in this way birth and death can be understood as the events in which we pass from one vibration frequency, and hence from one world, to another . . . [115]

A reader with a different intellectual background will seek out other attempts at an explanation, related to the symbols of his own conceptions. Some of the dying have been able to fit their experience without any difficulty into the Christian view of dying. The important thing seems to me, in following up these things, not to set up one doctrine against another. For this is part of our way of asserting ourselves. Dying frees us from that. If we want to extract a demonstrable doctrine out of what has been communicated to us here, the attempt will hardly pay off. Most of what we have heard is too vague and indistinct. Truths that can be formulated were not revealed. The content of the truth our spirit receives in dying and death it can probably only grasp when it has reached the heights of the state of knowledge that is appropriate to that truth, when it is no longer the numbers and figures familiar to us which, as Novalis put it, 'are the keys of all created being . . . : when light and shadow can once more come together to form true clarity.'

Our words only toil laboriously after these matters. We certainly sense that these accounts are those of an experience that demands of us what goes beyond thought. I have only been able to draw attention to these five points. The reader may find many more. Where do we come from? Where are we going to? Who is man? Whatever mankind's philosophies and religions say about these things that is important and true is given life and depth through the experiences of the dying. I have to consider anew words like original sin, basic guilt, and *karma*, transmigration of souls, foreknowledge, the Last Judgement, the forgiveness of sins, purification, justification, redemption, paradise, and *nirvana*—all the great symbols in which we try to apprehend human existence. I have to consider them anew if only because I have learnt that we do not only have to die; we are, above all, permitted to die; that as created beings we have no need to shudder at death, but that in dying fear is taken from us.

What Comes Afterwards

Our informants have returned from the threshold of death. They have seen death close to, but they did not take the final step over the threshold. We said at the beginning that it is impossible to say anything about death. We cannot incorporate it into life, cannot understand it in the light of life, for death is life's contradiction. But no reader of these accounts will fail all the same to ask whether we cannot draw any conclusions from them about death and what comes after death.

Modern Christian theology stresses the radical nature of death and the deadness of a person in his death. It does not have the Bible unequivocally on its side in this respect, but it finds the argument convenient for faith's sake. If I rest all my hope on God alone, trusting that he will raise me from the dead, then I must not be permitted to believe simultaneously that I can preserve part of myself beyond death.

This makes Christianity the contrary of Platonic philosophy. According to the latter, body and soul are divided at death. The soul, the good and noble principle, leaves what is imperfect—the body—behind it on earth and rises to a new, eternal life with God. We all know that this idea has dominated the whole of western history and is hardly to be expelled from our minds even today. But now not only modern Christian theology, but contemporary anthropology as well (the scientific teaching about man) has its difficulties with this concept.

We have seen that science recognises as the object of its research only the animated body and only a soul that is bound to bodily organs and works together with them. Man is the melody that sounds by means of the organ and its player. Neither of the two must be lacking, neither of the two is conceivable by itself when we think of human life—neither the musician nor the organ. Either of them, taken alone, is dead, indeed never existed, as many scientists believe. The Bible too knows man primarily as the unity of body and soul. Death affects the whole person; it shatters a person in both body and soul.

And yet Scripture does not speak unequivocally about what 'is' after death. It only testifies repeatedly to one thing: everyone is dead who is not with God, who is unable to praise God. In this way a person can be literally dead even though he is alive. Yahweh and the realm of the dead are mutually exclusive. Whoever is there cannot be with God. Death is absolute remoteness from God, God-forsakenness. But this is not to be interpreted as if it were a state. How long death 'lasts', how long, according to Christian belief, a person may be remote from God when he is dead is theological speculation.

Modern Christian theology stresses the caesura of death too sharply. It suggests the notion that the person lies in the realm of the dead—i.e., in remoteness from God, destroyed body and soul, as whole person and as person wholly—until a Last Judgement, when Christ will put the individual and all mankind together again, body and soul, in a new human life. For faith's sake, theology wants to prevent our making the transition too easy. Death is not like changing horses, as Ludwig Feuerbach put it.[116] It is the end of all our concepts, because from this frontier onwards, our consciousness knows neither space nor time.

The Platonic view of man cannot be maintained in this simplicity. In face of the data with which the psychology and psychiatry of our own day provides us, we cannot accept that man is divided into two parts, body and soul. Scientifically the matter is much more complicated, to say the least. Division between body and soul is only an image for a process which we cannot grasp. But the supposition that body and soul will be put together again in the resurrection—even the complete new creation of the whole person which is then accepted by modern theologians—is only an image as well.

But images are not a matter of indifference. We ought to decide in favour of the image that corresponds to the concept of man which our religious conviction offers us and which science cannot contradict. But my religious convictions are not purely arbitrary either. I want to be able to live with them. They must bind me into a life which can make me whole and free for new life.

The doctrine that when a person dies no 'eternal soul' is left behind (a doctrine upheld in radical form by Karl Barth) can neither be proved nor disproved in the light of science. Nor is this theology's concern. Psychology says that it can observe psychic life in its object (the living person) only in conjunction with organic life; and perhaps for this reason it is a matter of course among most of its practitioners to assume that psychic life cannot endure by itself beyond death. But this is merely the assumption of these psychologists, just as the assertion of an 'eternal soul' would be an assumption. Here we are in the realm of belief.

I, at least, have never found it a satisfactory idea that with death the whole man ceases to be and becomes nothing, in order then to be called and reconstituted anew on Judgement Day from the Creator's memory, as whole person in his physical and spiritual existence. I can come to terms neither with the assumption of an intermediate vacuum, nor with the assumption that the identical person, after his total disintegration in this separation from his earthly predecessor, will suddenly arise anew, at the sound of the Last Trump. The mythological thinking that is otherwise so despised today seems to me to be at work here.

This doctrine is consistent and self-contained and is widely supported today. But not only does it paralyse my faith, not only does it stand in contradiction to observations I have made and convictions I have gained in other fields; it cannot be harmonised with important New Testament statements either. According to the New Testament, we can far more readily accept belief in a person's fellowship with God immediately after his death (Luke 20.38; Phil. 1.23; John 11.25).

The Scriptures hold death to be the discontinuance of our earthly existence. It makes it impossible for us to hide ourselves any longer from the divine truth or to hinder the revelation of our own truth. But for that very reason it is not the end of my individual pilgrimage. On the contrary, this journey through death is taken really seriously for the first time. The devout man of the Old Covenant believes that God 'does not give his soul up to death' (Ps. 16.10; Acts 2.27), that God '[lifteth]me up from the gates of death' (Ps. 9.13).

Even a psychology which holds the soul to be a function of the brain must face up to the question, what man then really is, if, when his body is destroyed, his mental and spiritual life thereby perishes. And theology cannot overlook the biblical statements, according to which the dead have a history. Of course it is obvious that the word history for the 'time' after death is totally inappropriate, since death brings with it the end of space and time for those who have died. But we simply only possess words from our three-dimensional world. Every word about death and the dead, about eternal life and resurrection, is only an image. Yet we cannot just hold our tongues about the dead. They don't merely fall into a pit, to stay there till the resurrection.

I have often said that the experiences of the dying that have been passed on to us have no conclusive force. They can be put aside as products of the disturbed imagination of someone in a coma. Perhaps someone will make this an explanation of the fact that they all (in spite of individual deviations) talk such a uniform, unanimous language. But anyone who allows the reports to convince him that death cannot be very different, if dying is like this, is not entitled to think, for instance, that knowledge of this kind could save him from having to believe. My belief that death is not my permanent destiny, my hope that God will not let a moment pass before taking me to himself, beyond death, as Jesus promised the thief on the cross (Luke 23.43), my faith that hopes for a new existence beyond death—this is the primary thing. It is founded on the promise that Christ gave and which he himself is. But when theological speculation sets out to describe dying, death, and the life beyond in detail, then it will be permissible for me to draw on experiences from another sphere, in order to make more comprehensible to myself, among the many possible images of these inconceivable things, that image which corresponds to my faith and frees me from the unnecessary obligation to think along particular lines.

Modern theology rightly tries to avoid Platonic dualism. But at this point it countenances dualism; it splits the person and his world. Death is supposed to destroy him radically—literally, destroy him with his very roots; the new birth of the future resurrection is to allow him to come into being again, out of nothing. Where 'was' the Lord in the three days when his crucified body was lying in the tomb? Where 'was' he, until he took on the new body which Paul calls the 'spiritual body' (1 Cor. 15.44)? Or was he not, was he nothing?

At the risk of coming somewhat close to the Platonic heresy at this point, I am unable to believe that the human personality perishes in death. And personality means among other things the efficacy of the spirit that strives towards perfection, entelechy. We continue to be, spiritually, beyond death. The Christian Church began to think about the dead Christ very early on, until the idea developed that he, the One who was dead, descended to the dead in order to preach salvation to them during these three days (1 Peter 3.19f.; 4.6). This may not be the most important tenet of my faith, but in this context it is important. It tells me something about the destiny of the person I shall one day be when I die.

Dying, as we have generally been taught—dying in fear and horror, dying in an agonising coming to terms with my past, the terrible severance of body and soul, dying as punishment and judgement—all this fits better into the modern doctrine of radical discontinuance. But what the experiences of the dying themselves allow us to guess: that is to say, that dying lets the person step outside but without being shattered, expands and sublimates him, frees him from the pressing constraint of the tunnel passages; dying like this brings us nearer to faith in transformation, exaltation, migration of the spirit, and new life. When the apostle talks, as we have just heard, about our being in the resurrection 'a spiritual body', he expresses in this paradox the difficulty of talking about our new existence. It is true that our spirit will be bound to a body as it was in our earthly life. But we cannot understand this new body as being an equation of our present one, with skin and sinews and nerves, let alone as being the same body that we immured, broken and decaying, in the churchyard grave.

Our accounts share this difficulty. They speak several times about the fact that this self, which endures throughout the experience of dying, even when the brain in the abandoned body sinks into darkness, moves towards, or even arrives at, a new dimension. The narrators have only been able to talk about this in stammering terms. As long as we communicate with other living beings, we are in the third dimension and talk in its images. But it would all the same be foolish, just because of that, to doubt the possibility of further dimensions, states, and conditions of existence.

Every higher dimension, however, incorporates the lower one. Area absorbs what is merely linear, volume absorbs area. Mathematics guesses, at most, how space-time is exceeded. The lower is commensurable with the higher dimension, but not vice versa. That is why we do not here see and hear and grasp the spiritual world into which we penetrate after death, but which is invisibly present in our present world. For there is only a single world, God's *one* world.

A theology that aims not at division but at unity will have no difficulty here. We never grasp the whole of God's single world. Our consciousness separates out only one part of it, our own reality; it sets bounds to one sector of God's limitless world, and temporalises only one time out of his eternity. With death we shall be set free of our frontiers. But we cannot detach ourselves from God, who is the whole. He envelops us in every form which our spirit achieves and which is in Christ.

And according to the apostle he will envelop even more closely the person who has passed through death into that other dimension of his efficacy. Teilhard de Chardin stresses again and again that 'In an atmosphere of pure love God will be "all in all" (1 Cor. 12.6)'. That is not pantheism. For pantheism, God and the world coincide. The Christian, on the other hand, believes that the world has been created by God out of nothing—and has been created through his Word. That means that it was dismissed to freedom and responsibility. Consequently we do not return through death to the great stream of phenomena, as the pantheistic heaven promises. 'We shall rather be taken up again by the divine power, be taken hold of, dominated—the power which is included in the forces of inner dissolution, which is above all present in the irresistible longing which sweeps our separated soul along the paths of its destiny in the beyond, in as natural a necessity as the way the vapour rises when the sun shines over the water. Death delivers us up wholly to God; it lets us enter into him. But on the other hand we must deliver ourselves up to death in immense love and self-giving.'[117]

We have read in the accounts of the dying about these forces of inner dissolution—the dissolution which is present in the longing for the new union: like the grain of salt which dissolves in the sea, we were told. The theologian puts it in this way: 'The liberation of man from death will not take place through any journey of the body through space. The spirit must, without regret, leave what is left of life to space, and must leave it behind—once having reached maturity—in order to seek, not another, visible star, but the higher, limitless unity of the universe, the single core which surrounds the whole spirit, yet without imprisoning it.'[118]

The Spirit World and the Spirits

But cannot we also bring forward the depositions of witnesses as to what comes afterwards? Here the door to occultism is wide open. No less a man than Arthur Schopenhauer roundly agreed to the possibility that the dead communicate with us, putting it down to what he defined as their 'animal magnetism'. It must be possible, he thought, for a person to recognise—recognise directly, by means of the brain—figures in visible form who are outside space and time. For space and time are, after all, in the Idealist view of the world which Schopenhauer maintained, only the forms of appearance under which the world is revealed to our sensory organs.[119]

Joy Snell, an English nurse, in her book *The Ministry of Angels, Here and Beyond*[120] tells the story of her life as being a complete chain of appearances by the dead, visitations of bright and dark angels at the bed of the sick. From the age of twelve, this woman had physical contact with figures from the beyond in which she believed. As a nurse, she watched at many death-beds and discovered in herself the gift of recognising dying and the moment when the dying leave their bodies. 'Angels of salvation' appeared to her and supported her in her nursing. She was able to experience beforehand in visions the death of people who were near and dear to her as well as the recovery of patients whom the doctors had given up. According to her account, she often left the earth 'as spirit' in radiant form, in order to view the glories of 'the other world'. She described this other world in highly concrete and vivid terms as an idyllic, heavenly garden. The reader is reminded in reading of Emanuel Swedenborg's visions. The comparison with this Swede (1688–1772), whom contemporaries called 'the Columbus of science', indicates how fluid the transition is from the ecstatically visionary to occult clairvoyance.

There are testimonies from both sectors: it would not be difficult to follow up the accounts of the dying with an equally long list of accounts given by the dead. But the aim of our present book does not lie in this direction. We want to help to get rid of erroneous ideas about dying, not to describe the world beyond. When a person dies his dying is still part of this world, which is apprehensible by the senses. The so-called super-sensory world, into which mediums have insight, is a subject of its own which we can only touch on here. A few indications for the reader's guidance must suffice.

The experiences of the dying we have been considering in this book derive from the people who have gone through these experiences. However we judge them, they remain the authentic testimonies of these men and women. They have experienced dying as a process in their own minds or souls. Spiritualism rests on testimonies of a different kind. It believes that men and women go on living after death and is convinced that an exchange between the world of the living and the world of the dead is possible. Our atmosphere, it claims, is full of 'spiritual' emanations from the dead, and everyone has an organ through which they can be received. As with a radio transmitter, it simply has to be tuned in to the wave-length on which the dead transmit. This wave-length is the unconscious.

And now spiritualism tries to tune in its mediums to this correct wave-length. This practice of calling up the dead is as old as mankind itself and is becoming highly popular again, in spite of all efforts at elucidation. The mediums must have, or must develop, the capacity for shutting out their everyday consciousness; they must be able to separate body and soul in order to make their unconscious the mouthpiece of the dead. Whereas in dying an intensified consciousness of the self develops—a kind of super-consciousness in which the person acquires clarity about himself—in spiritualism the self of the spiritualistic medium must be blotted out, so that a dead person can take possession of this consciousness and speak through the mouth of this person

The method is questionable and dangerous. It has been emphatically warned against from time immemorial by all who have been concerned for man's welfare. Yet, in the face of the overwhelming number of testimonies from all periods, it cannot seriously be denied that it is possible for a person to be possessed by another spirit: by spirits, demons, angels, and the dead. The Gospel itself offers many examples. We must only be clear about the fact that all these are psychic experiences. What the medium communicates merely presents us with the spiritual reflection of another world, concealed in our own. In order to become communication, it must use our methods of speech.

We should all like to have the confirmation that this other world exists. But the question is wrongly formulated. For 'to exist' in the sense of being present, something we come across, is only conceivable in the space of the three-dimensional environment of our world 'on this side'. No-one can prove a 'world beyond' by parapsychological data,[121] and if the dead speak through mediums we still only have the language of the medium at our disposal, and that belongs to our present world of time and space. The term 'parapsychology' is an apt one: in all spiritualistic phenomena, even the apparently most incomprehensible ones, it is a matter of the soul's walking 'alongside itself', as the word suggests.

The step from knowledge to faith may in this way be moved outwards a little further, but we are not saved from taking the step itself. And it must be added that the spiritualistic evocations of the dead have up to now brought us no serious knowledge. What the dead have said through the lips of mediums has usually been extremely trivial, so that one might well reach the conclusion that only the dead who cling especially closely to earthly existence and who are still unable to detach themselves from their petty wants can be conjured up by spiritualistic means. It is in line with this supposition that most reports of appearances by the dead concern people who have only died shortly before and are still, as it were, in the psychic vicinity of the living who are aware of them.

The difference between the key-hole metaphysics of the spiritual-

ists and the visions of the world beyond experienced by Swedenborg, Joy Snell, the medieval women ecstatics Elisabeth von
Schönau, Birgitta von Schweden, Gertrud von Helfta, Marina von
Escobar, or whoever we like to name out of the great chorus, lies
precisely at the point where we have already discovered the difference between the experiences of the dying and the experiences of
drug addicts: in the one group the consciousness diminishes, as it
were, and strives towards its unconsciousness, its vacuum; in the
other, among the dying and visionaries, the consciousness reaches
beyond itself into what we have called super-consciousness.

Spiritualism, moreover, only interrogates individual dead persons
by means of the hypnotised medium; it lets the dead be conjured up
in order to extract some information from them. This is the pro-
ceeding which cost King Saul his throne. In his fear of the Philis-
tines, he wanted to speak to the dead priest and prophet Samuel
through the witch of Endor (1 Sam.28). Inquisitive dealings of this
kind with the dead, via oracles (common practice among races since
ancient times) is strictly forbidden by the Bible. Here man seeks
revelation from below by devious paths, whereas it has long since
been available to him in the Word of God.

But this does not mean that the eye of faith is not also granted
insight into a spirit world belonging to a different dimension from
our own. The Bible, both Old and New Testaments, is full of such
accounts of the 'translation' of prophets who looked upon the
heavens, the realm of the dead, and the future. But in this biblical
'spiritualism' a single soul is never seen. The heavenly host who
have been redeemed from death are looked upon as a company.
And in exactly the same way, the long chain of believing ecstatics
of Christendom has seen 'the world hereafter', 'the kingdom
above', as a company of souls, not in their isolation and their lonely
wanderings. The Church below contemplates the Church above
and lives in correspondence with it.

This is so in all the great religions. The religious spiritualist, the
man of spiritual vision, sees unity among the worlds and unity in
man, on this side of death as well as beyond it, 'here below and
there above'. He makes no dogmatic division into 'this life' and the
beyond but unites them, in his vision, into a single world. The

'afterwards' is already present in our believing acceptance of it. The person cannot die, for his spirit is part of this unity, or rather, not part of it but the unity itself. 'So mightily has man been created', wrote Paracelsus, 'that he is more than heaven and earth. Man and the heavens are one thing.'[122] Two hundred years later Swedenborg took up these ideas again in his doctrine of *homo maximus*, the cosmic man, who is 'spiritual matter' or 'materialized spirit'. Among the eastern religions, Jainism preaches the same doctrine.[123]

The modern materialistic and biological philosophy of life, in line with the dominating theory of descent, holds that the highest is the product of the lowest and that the spirit is the end-product of evolution out of matter. This suggests the idea that this highest development also disappears again in the death of the lower one, by which it is supported. In the Indian religions, and in the broad stream of Christian mysticism and spiritualism which has accompanied the Church since its early days down to contemporary anthroposophy, the idea is the reverse one. Here the highest life is the primal one and the origin of the spirit, the proto-form and archetype, and from the very beginning the idea towards which all forms of life strive. This great idea is shared by such different thinkers as Plato and Hegel, Leibniz and Fichte, Paracelsus and Goethe, Swedenborg and Jakob Böhme, Eckehart, Tauler and Joachim da Fiore, Sebastian Franck and Casper von Schwenckfeldt, Nicholas of Cusa and Teilhard de Chardin; here Vedanta, early monasticism, and romanticism all meet. And here there are no difficulties about the life 'hereafter'. For the spirit which is the origin and the goal, and which forms matter in its own image, cannot be thought of in mortal terms. Anyone who partakes of it cannot perish. In this great mansion of the spiritualists, in the true sense the adorers of the spirit for whom death is, in Swedenborg's words, 'a continuation of life and a mere transition',[124] our contemporary spiritualists have only rented a pitiful little room. They get excited about appearances of the dead which for the others are a matter of course.

It was for them, *these* spiritualists, the men and women of little faith among the adherents of the spirit, who believe in the world of spirits more than in the spirit world, that Jesus once told the folk tale about the rich man, Dives, and the poor man, Lazarus. After his death, the angels immediately carried Lazarus off to Abraham's bosom, whereas Dives went to the dead who were suffering in eternal fire. Dives could see Lazarus from a long way away, and knew how well off he was. So he called to Father Abraham and asked him to send Lazarus to bring him a drop of water, so that he could cool himself. When this was refused, Dives begged that Lazarus might at least be sent to his five brothers to warn them, lest they too went to hell. But Abraham (who was steward in Paradise, according to this Jewish legend) answered: 'They have Moses and the prophets; let them hear them ... If they do not hear Moses and the prophets, neither will they be convinced if some one should rise from the dead' (Luke 16. 29ff.).

5. THE CONSEQUENCES

The Consequences for Doctors and Clergy

Anyone who tries to come to terms with the experiences of the dying will want to examine not only what he has learnt but also his own reactions to dying and his dealings with dying people. The criticism we levied at the beginning of the book against society's practice has been confirmed. If dying is the most splendid experience bestowed on man, we ought to give it a different place in our lives. This applies in the first instance to the place where most people die nowadays: the hospital.

We push the great affair of dying away from us. The person who is said to be 'failing' is left to himself. Our informants, on the other hand, tell us again and again that now, having returned, they draw on this experience and feel they have to think about it continually. How would it be if dying and death were also thought about far more by the people who, in our society, are generally the ones who impose it or simply let it happen, or who accept it, in anger or resignation, as the failure of their skill? The doctor-as-mechanic is a product of our present society. Society teaches its young people many things, but no-one talks about dying and death in our schools and universities. There are no evening classes in this important subject. Even the new 'meditation' wave has not managed to achieve that. Our medical students rightly learn to distinguish between types of schizomycete and how to sew up a wound neatly. But they hear nothing about dying in their lectures. This is where the registrar or chief medical officer stops short. As doctor, he neither can nor will tell his students how they should deal with the dying in his hospital, except as regards their actual medical care.

The nurses and orderlies have the main burden of the dying and the dead. But where the sick person's most important question is concerned—the question about his true condition—their lips are sealed. The result of long discussions about 'truth at the sick bed' has mainly been a prohibition: it must not be left to these 'lower auxiliaries'. The nurse has to leave it to the doctor to decide whether or not he will say 'it' and when. If our society were more aware that dying is no reason for fear, and involves no pain but merely opens doors, it would surely also have to fulfil its duty to tell the truth in a totally different way. And not only in hospital. For the sake of a death of this kind, I can learn quite early on that I have cancer. I have no need to be ashamed because I am going to die earlier than other people. On the contrary, I have reason to rejoice. The sooner I know 'it', the more time I have to think about the joy and to arrange my life with that in view. I can begin to work at 'my own' dying all the sooner; but we shall be talking about this in the final section.

All the people who have dealings with the dying ought first of all to adopt a simple rule which experienced doctors have always known and which is confirmed by the accounts of the dying them-selves: 'The dying person is "conscious" much longer than one thinks: one must always reckon with his hearing and understand-ing.'[125] We have already seen that the dying person may not seem to hear, and perhaps really cannot do so, since he does not answer. He may not even give any sign with his eyes any more, and has already ceased to be able to move his hands. All the same, he has not yet become our 'object'. If we are to believe the reports of the dying, his consciousness has rather reached a new dimension, but it continues to be aware of this one for a long time. He perceives truth about his surroundings, whereas what we perceive about him is false. It is the sense of touch, above all, that remains to the end. Those who have returned have repeatedly told how distinctly they felt touch and the pressure of the hand. It was his friends' hands especially that Eckart Wiesenhütter 'experienced' first of all, when he returned. On his death bed the doctor could think about his hands, with which he was supposed to carry out medical treatment (to 'handle' his patients) and had once done so. The clergy and the nurses can learn to speak through the careful touch of their hands. They may be certain that the dying person will understand.

But our accounts have now made it probable that our talk about 'comforting the dying' is ill chosen in most cases. In the final phase the dying person is withdrawn from our comfort. Our encouragement cannot hold him back. And the presupposition behind the encouragement we usually give is false. The poor chap in the bed there has no need of our compassion. On the contrary, he is nearer a joy for which we shall perhaps have to wait ardently for a long time. It lies with us whether we can go a little way with the person who is dying. We do not have to lead him; he leads us.

It is necessary and possible for us to make an about-turn. When we are with a dying person, we are always imagining what he must be feeling like. Seeing him dying from the outside, we fit him into our psychological world, which is a world greedy for life and mad to possess, a machine for having, not a mode of being. But he has been withdrawn from this world, or is on the way to being so, and everything would depend on our seeking to be with him, by recognising what is really happening to him, what he himself is saying. That we can guess anyway, after having read our reports.

In dying the two 'worlds' are still mutually pervaded. Perception of one's surroundings has not as yet been completely blotted out, and the self has already escaped to the greater vision of life through the 'tunnel' into the light. The self's perception of its surroundings is indeed immensely sharpened, since the body no longer offers any resistance. In this phase the sick person thinks he can hear a goods train pounding away above his head, because the matron didn't manage to persuade her probationers not to wear clogs, or because the door slammed again.

We attribute to the dying person our own reactions and our notions about a normal person. We put the inner equilibrium of a normal person on a level with the disturbed equilibrium of the dying person and then decide that the Great Reaper has already laid his hands on the dying person's capacity for perception, which is suffering from this arrhythmical condition. In this way we analyse with our intelligence a condition which lies beyond our reason and our logic—we analyse the dying with our brain. Once more we see how the human mind, imprisoned in the cage of his sensory perceptions, is incapable of thinking contrary to appearances.[126]

After even these few indications it becomes obvious to us that there is much that needs altering in our way of dealing with the dying, if there is to be any talk about 'standing by them'. We certainly stand by them, but quite helplessly. The hospital must learn to have a completely different respect for them. The tender services with which we surround them ought to be based on a much better understanding of the process of dying. We need seminars everywhere to teach people how to deal with the dying. These should not immediately offer techniques—less than is otherwise the case in medicine—but should first of all try to illuminate the psychical background of dying, which will enable us to find a deeper human understanding. We shall only gain access to a new technique of dealing with the dying in the light of our knowledge of this background.

Almost everything we have heard about dying in this book admonishes the medicine of our time to recognise its limitations. A man or woman is not a machine whose parts have to be repaired by the doctor if they are working badly. He or she is a meaningful unity between life and death. Dying is not a disaster. That is why the doctors must be humbler and give up their enmity towards dying as a biological fact. The patient is not an object; he is a person before God. His death is much more than a biological fact. Paracelsus, who was himself a great physician, formulated the tenet: 'The patient is the doctor and the doctor is his assistant.' Was he a great physician because this is the way he thought?

In this book we have entered into the possibility of inner experience in dying. Medicine which respects this will have to have a quite different approach to the terminal phase from the one found today in our mammoth hospitals. It will talk the doctors out of the authoritative behaviour and the group arrogance which isolates them, not only from the nurses but from the patients too. It will at last insist on their sharing the explanation of his illness with the patient, so as to make his co-operation and self-help possible. Medicine of this kind will no longer cut itself off protectively from the act of dying but, together with the patient, for him but for the doctor too, take up the task of practising dying together.[127]

Here I should like to underline everything which Elisabeth Kübler-Ross has written in her book *On Death and Dying*[128] about dealing with people who are *facing* death. For the dying phase itself, which is the subject of the present book, the following also applies, and applies above all: when they are face to face with dying, the doctor, the psychotherapist, the nurse, and the priest or pastor certainly come to the end of their usual practice, and even of their most super-modern pastoral dialogue; but they have not come to the end altogether, not to the end of all potential help. All the demands I have mentioned apply to the pastor in the doctor and the nurse and to the professional priest or minister. For the body is after all incapable of being nursed and healed if we take it to be without a spirit. This is what most of our specialists still do, unfortunately, and are probably forced to do, so as to be in time to ring for the next patient. Medicine seems to flourish in the process. But that is its undoing.

The minister or priest, however, who for his part sees only the soul and not the body, as if man on this side of the threshold were to be seen as anything but a unity, is no less helpless in the face of the dying. During his studies, the future clergyman gets to know particular procedures which the Church performs for the dying. They are of a venerable liturgical kind. But the student is not told how the priest or pastor treats the dying person who is no longer accessible for the message of the forgiveness of sins. Later, but sooner than he thinks, he will stand at the bedside of someone who is dying. His faith is challenged when the doctor says to him: 'You take over. I can't do any more. But of course the patient doesn't know.'[129]

Perhaps the clergyman is now soon at the end of his resources too. Then he generally puts on a liturgical mask, embarrassed and horrified. This will be the case if he knows his dogmatics and has learnt that death is the wages of sin and is man's enemy, but does *not* know what is happening within the dying person as he dies, and how he can stay beside him in body and soul, even when the dying person does not seem to understand anything any more. Then he only has the relevant biblical texts and hymns at his disposal. Many experiences show that it is certainly far from unprofitable to call texts to the unconscious mind of the dying person, texts which have helped him in critical situations before, or even texts which mean something to him in general and which waken the buried world of faith. It is rightly often regretted that the contemporary man, in his quickly growing alienation from faith and the Church, is familiar with fewer and fewer of these texts, with which our fathers were able not only to live but also to die. What can he tell himself that retains validity 'in that last hour', when there is nothing more to say? For everyone who does not die the blessed death of Abraham, the question of life's meaning remains oppressively open in this final hour. Only one assurance can give comfort that remains valid even when existence fails. Not many of our contemporaries are responsive to an assurance of this kind.

When nothing else helps, when it is too late for spiritual help through words, let alone for today's modern dialogistic pastoral care, the priest or minister tries to pray with the person who is dying. If even this is no longer possible, he prays for him and over him, as was the custom in the early Church. But this too can only have meaning when the dying person is still at home in this world of faith. He must be someone who hears the voice coming from the other side. There are no prayers in Christianity which have a mechanical effect. Most of the things which we say at the deathbed are an admission of our helplessness.

But I think that this admission should be made. The accounts given by the dying could teach us that it is not as important as we always thought for us to do something for the person who is dying. We must rather endure the silence and try to remain with him in that silence by means of our accompanying presence which, though for us he is unconscious, he now consciously experiences as the approach to the point where a person becomes completely true.

Pastoral care at the bedside of the sick and dying must come to deal with that dimension of truth in this moment of crisis. The person who is given the pastoral charge will be dependent on the situation in the hospital and on the disposition and the wish of the patient especially. It can be the doctor, the nurse, a relative, or a clergyman. The last of these may have the professional qualifications, but he has no exclusive privilege. He will have no desire to appear on the scene in the final hour like a magician who, at the very last minute, puts everything right by means of some spell. But whoever it is that sits at the bedside, he has to take over the task of helping to remove the fear, that mistaken encumbrance of dying. This fear could spring up at the very moment when the truth about the approaching end of earthly life has to be disclosed.

This means among other things that the pastor will not participate in the modern way of doing things which was described at the beginning. He will expressly remove death's tabu. He will have no part in repressing the idea of death, nor will he make light of it. He will neither reproduce death's nightmare spectres nor rob it of its dignity. He will be beside the dying person with the assurance and cheerfulness which faith confers and yet without wanting to convey the plump, self-satisfied clerical certainty which is not aware that there are any questions left. For after all he knows no more than the dying person does; he has at best the experience behind him which the dying person is now going through, because he knows about so many other people who have died in faith. For him, therefore, humility and patience are the most valuable virtues. It is obvious that they cannot be practised as part of the hospital routine, in an eight-hour day. For that reason alone, the institution of the full-time hospital chaplain, whose sole function is supposed to be providing comfort from morning to night, has its difficulties.

It would in fact be much more desirable if this task could be laid on many shoulders. But this will only be possible when new knowledge about the true nature of dying becomes available to wide groups of people, when the whole staff of our hospitals is initiated into it, and when the truth about dying finds entry into families. Most of us still cut ourselves off from the dying, because we avoid death as our personal, anonymous enemy and see it as punishment, the wrath of God, loneliness. We have said what there is to be said about this. These arguments may come to the fore in the early stages of dying, but our accounts have shown that its last phase is dominated by another, brighter mood, which is, in my view, the reality of dying. Where it is accepted, a man can more easily bear to sit beside his dying fellow. Someone who is not moving towards inexorable darkness (as we have always thought) but is travelling towards the light will no longer be the object of our compassion; he might even be cause for envy. We will then act differently on his behalf and will stay beside him in a different state of mind from before.

In this book we are talking only about the very last hour of dying. Now the pastor or priest who is with the dying person has the 'truth' which has to be told at the sick bed behind him. The dying patient has come face to face with the fact of his dying. He cannot be fooled about anything any more. We need not discuss in detail here at what point someone who is incurably ill should be told the truth, or how long the merciful lies should be imposed on him for the sake of the last, despairing hope of his survival. But we see that this question too takes on a totally new form if dying is what we have described it as being. Pastoral care, it seems to me, is not possible without the imposition of truth, even truth that seems bitter; for pastoral care aims at leading the person into truth. And how can it do this if it is dealing in lies?

This brings many new tasks for doctors and clergy. In recent years the beginnings of a psychotherapy for the dying have been developed, first in the United States and later in Europe as well. Doctors and theologians try in fruitful co-operation to help the person in his last hours by leading him to accept the meaning of his life in its unique, once-for-all character. In doing this they are not interested in the dying patient because he is dying or because he is a patient, but 'because he has the right to be treated as a personality to the very last'.[130] That is to say, pastoral care for a person because he is dying and in that he is dying—a pastoral care that does not look back into life but forward into death—is still lacking. It will only be

possible when we summon up the courage as priest or pastor to
look into death as it really is and to accompany the dying person
into dying as he experiences it.

Euthanasia

This brings us to the subject which is causing such public concern
today. I understand by euthanasia everything that has just been
said; there is no better way of helping the dying towards an easy
death than the things we have discussed: pastoral care that looks
squarely at dying; information about dying as the dying themselves
have experienced it; the breaking down of our fear and avoidance of
the bogeyman we have created for ourselves; the stripping the gods
of death of their divinity; a humble accompanying of the dying into
their pregnant silence; and the hope for my own dying. The dying
will be helped if our hospitals should one day look different; if the
sick and the doctors cease to talk about dying each in their separate
groups, but talk openly about it together; and if doctors, nurses,
and theologians have learnt during their training that a person's
dying is to be accepted as his life's final achievement and as a
splendid, great, and liberating experience. Once they have recognised this, and if they live with their own deaths, they will know
how to deal with the dying.

Today, however, euthanasia is understood almost exclusively as
the problem in the greyish zone between medicine and crime which
many people now want the law to regulate: should life be pro-
longed in all circumstances or may it be curtailed in certain cases to
help the patient? I do not want to intervene in this difficult discussion, but should only like to point out the consequences that
emerge here too from the other view of dying which this book
offers. In the United States, in Japan, Denmark, Holland, Great
Britain, and Switzerland strong citizens' action groups are fighting
to get passive and active euthanasia exempted from punishment.
Euthanasia is passive when the doctor dispenses with the appli-
cation of life-prolonging measures and remedies in the case of a
terminal patient. Active euthanasia is the killing of an incurably ill
patient who is tormented by unbearable pain, at his express and

earnest desire. At its General Meeting on 12 December 1974, the Baden-Württemberg Medical Council passed the following resolution on this problem:

1. Every person has the unconditional right to his natural death.
2. The doctor respects the limitations to which his actions are subject.
3. The doctor cannot be required to prolong the life of a dying person where this only means an artificial and useless postponement of an unavoidable end.
4. Apart from this, the relief of pain and torment remains a fundamental medical duty.

But in the misery of our overcrowded intensive care units, it may well be difficult to draw the line between passive and active euthanasia. All too often, pain-relieving narcotics also shorten life. Moreover the declaration of the Baden-Württemberg doctors also avoids the essential problem. For we do not know what 'natural death' is. So we do not know what we are saying when we demand our right to it. I am inclined to call death 'natural' at most if it makes it possible for dying to be the kind of experience that finds expression in our accounts. But every death is different and the experience cannot be forced or organised. I can only guess that dying of this kind is prevented in the case of countless men and women—doctors claim it is by far the greater proportion—who, being in coma, are reduced to the zero-point of consciousness through drugs. And I am neither desirous for anyone one day to cut short my dying process in this way; nor do I want my helpless body to have a final period of vegetation forced on it when it is no longer able to achieve the act of living. We have already seen in the case of Lev Landau how terrible, agonising, and senseless such triumphs of medical technique are for the victim. One day I should like to be able to give myself into the hands that are awaiting me. Today medicine can prolong life practically indefinitely. But it seldom knows what the point of prolonging it is. The problem is not so much the euthanasia of the incurably ill as a medical skill in the prolongation of life which has arrived at perfection. This skill can, formally speaking, take its stand on the Hippocratic oath, which compels it to act in this way. But helping, healing actions especially must not be allowed to separate the body from the person, or the vegetative life from the spiritual one. Psychosomatically informed society must find a way whereby man is freed from the fatal adoration of his biological life and accepts his destiny, which includes dying and death. And we have seen from so many examples that dying does not have to be terrible. It is only our fear of it that is terrible. Anyone who has ever been in Mother Theresa's homes for the dying in Calcutta or even in St Christopher's Hospice for the Dying in London knows that whether in prosperity here or in destitution there our problem of how to prolong life by the most cunning means seems highly eccentric and in fact undignified. I see another dimension when I look at the accounts the dying themselves have given us. Life is God's gift to me. But I am not identical with that life. So I can even leave it behind me when I am called.

Natural Death

The movement in favour of euthanasia, which has emerged among us with such élan, starts from the presupposition that the person knows what kind of death it is to which he is asserting his claims. Doctors and laymen call this death 'natural'. The aim is to die naturally. But according to everything that has been said in this book, we must not only put the word 'euthanasia' in inverted commas; we must do the same with 'natural death'.

If modern enlightened views wish contemporary people to have a 'natural death', the aim thereby is to give them the certainty that the whole business of dying can be settled in advance, once and for all. I live naturally—that means primarily in the affluent society. I have everything I want without limit, and can move freely in every direction. To die naturally would mean: I die as and when I have to. Since we have unfortunately not as yet abolished sickness, I will die when my disease becomes unbearable. I can provide for this by making a statement in the presence of a lawyer when I am still young; at last, this is what is demanded.

The best and therefore the most natural thing would consequently be for serious illness not to attack me at all. That would then be the most natural death of all, a death which is simply a matter of course, so to speak, an end without pain or effort, the finish which is simply the concomitant of life. The expression 'natural death' then means that this life has been lived to the finish, has come to the end to which it is entitled. Everyone, so the demand runs, has a right to a death like this. It is as undeniable a human right as—in the opinion of a growing number of our contemporaries—the right to bring about this death at a self-chosen moment if one so desires, supposing that nature does not accord it.

But really only the death of a being who is himself entirely nature can be truly natural—a being who is merely born, not called, merely creature, not creator, merely a species and a sex, not a person before the face of God. An animal certainly dies a natural death, provided it is still living in the environmental context proper to it. It simply perishes, as we say. The higher animals certainly have minds or souls. But they only arrive at mental consciousness, hardly at 'self' consciousness, and certainly not at a consciousness or sense of value. This soul will not step outside itself when it dies; it will not review and revise its history, that is to say, look at its history again in the life panorama; this soul will not be able to expand and see in dying the sunrise colours of the Eternal. But man's very definition as man means that he is never merely nature.

If his death is to be called natural, it cannot be something that is given to him and is his own. Man never 'has' a natural death. We have already seen that medicine uses this word, but is actually embarrassed when it does so.[131] It would like to be able to determine the cause of every death and actually manages to do so increasingly often. Really, medicine claims, no-one dies of old age; they die ultimately of some additional illness. We have just not yet always succeeded in discovering its name.

Natural death is therefore an understandable longing, but certainly not a matter of course. At this point in our progress, having come to know so many apparently easy deaths after what were possibly hard lives we can say that natural death belongs to the realm of paradise, the reconciled spirit, recovered childhood, the redeemed world. It stands under the covenant, beneath the seven-hued rainbow God spanned above the world after the flood-waters had gone down. Shall we become nature again in dying?

Freud saw death as the dissolution of the tension of the life instinct; faith may well make a different assumption: that in dying matter and spirit, nature and history, unite as, in Teilhard de Chardin's image, 'the molecules of our being are burst asunder. Death, Teilhard went on, 'is to provide the necessary entrance into our inmost selves. It will make us undergo the required dissociation.'[132] Death as the natural end of life could only be in prospect if we had death as a power in this life firmly under control. But that is a wish medicine can promise to fulfil, but whose fulfilment it cannot achieve. A world without death belongs to another dimension.

There is already talk about this dimension in the very first book of the Bible. The history of Israel's patriarchs finishes with the symbol of natural death that belongs to this paradisal order. It is natural death that is no doubt being claimed for the patriarch Abraham, who was 175 years old, the Scriptures say: 'Abraham breathed his last and died in a good old age, an old man and full of years, and was gathered to his people.' Job may have died a natural death, since we read that he too died 'an old man, and full of days', although the Bible only gives him 140 years. But both of them, Abraham and Job, were men who had earlier been tested to the uttermost. We cannot say that here a natural life was followed by a natural death. Here death is rather the fulfilment of a promise.

None of this is meant in any sense in which we understand the word nature today. In the Bible dying at 'a good old age' means dying in God, not a human right that can be legally claimed. The Bible uses this kind of death to express the design for a new person. Death among ourselves, as we are able to observe it from the outside, is of a different kind, as a rule. Our accounts tell us that only the dying person himself already looks a little way into this region, like a man who looks down a ride cut through a forest.

Overtaking Death

In the midst of life we experience death, we said at the beginning. In every separation we are separated from ourselves and think that what we are experiencing is an anticipation of the tearing apart of body and soul. Since we have now seen that this tearing apart does not bring with it the pain which we had always heard about, we shall also be able to acquire a new relationship to the separations which life imposes on us.

Now we shall learn to pay attention to the signs telling us that separation is not only loss and that the words of the burial service 'in the midst of life we are in death' does not bring a merely saddening message. The apostle longs to depart and to be with his Lord (Phil. 1.23), but he decides to remain for the sake of the people who are entrusted to him. Our accounts allow us to suppose that the separations inflicted on us are not hopelessly final.

Even before, this was the secret premise that made life possible. We experience what dying is before we die, but we do not actually die. With the first tear that we can weep over a grave, we testify that dying has for us no definitive meaning. Through our grief we let the dead go free, as it were; we move away from them by having them in a new way. The dead person is now someone whom we can mourn. Our first grief also contained the reproach that through him something within us had died. We get over this reproach. The dead person increasingly loses his position 'out there' among the host of the assembled dead—the position public burial has given him. He is more and more beside us.

He may be beside us, above all, with what he experienced in dying and is now experiencing in death. He is not in a worse position than us—he is ahead of us, and one day he will take us with him. Dying before we actually die is transformed into a positive value. Dying is not just utter loneliness, as we thought and were told. The stripping bare is not merely brutal. It liberates, releases, saves. The new stage is called unification through transformation.

We had always already outrun death in our lifetimes. We had always already had a notion that dying is 'gain'. For the ancient world, Dionysus was the recognition of the experience that nature leads us in the simplest way into the forecourts of the mystic tremor, in which dying and being born are simultaneously present. The grape, as symbol and gift of the god, is both Lethe and fire, forgetfulness and rapture. In every exaltation, in all fullness of life, death is present, secretly and unrecognised. But here life also takes the form of new life, as spirit and as love. We always saw only the one side: every incandescence is also loss, every intoxication is a secret appointment with our longing to die. Now we also recognise the reverse side of the shield: in losing I am caught up with; what goes ahead of me draws me ahead with it.

The beginning of dying, we said at the beginning, is our knowledge that dying exists. For this, after all, makes us people—that we cannot simply die, like animals—*ver-enden*, as German says. But now we see that we cannot 'end' either. If dying takes the form of my ceasing to remain in my body, which lies there unconscious, given up by the doctors, then my knowledge of dying before I die must acquire another form too. It is true that the leaves will continue to fall and that autumn will continue to have a metaphorical meaning for us; but we shall cease to look on flowers simply as things that are going to fade. If dying is not oppression, my knowledge that I am going to die will no longer oppress me. Instead of making me feel melancholy it will expand and deepen me. My will to live will not be weakened; on the contrary, I shall acquire a much deeper joy in life, because, knowing its limits, I look beyond them. Once we have overcome the fear of what comes at the end, life talks a new language. We then understand the poet for whom life becomes transparent in the contemplation of death:

When in the stillness of a summer evening
Through warm and golden air a leaf came down,
My wafted breath was in your shuddering,
My breath which to ripe things adheres; and when
A brimming-over and uprush of feeling
In a warm torrent flooded your trembling soul;
Or when a sudden spasm was revealing
Your kinship with the vast and the unknown,
And you, abandoned to the cosmic dance,
Received the whole world's rhythm as your own:
In every hour pregnant with more than chance
Experienced fully in your earthly station,
'Twas I who touched your very soul's foundation

With power most holy, fraught with mystery.[133]

If once we believed that life had turned to gall because, in its very midst, the breath of dying was so often wafted towards us, we now see that in this way the perceptions were already being formed through which clearer insight into the process of dying was mediated. This knowledge can only give us support. We shall no longer shrug our shoulders and talk about an inescapable fate. And when we are contemplating the world's misery and our own, we shall no longer be overcome (as we sometimes were earlier) by the faithless hope that one day, perhaps one day soon 'we shall be finished with it all'. The melancholy which so often accompanies the mature person will no longer paralyse him; it will support him and carry his joy in life down from the surface to the foundations of his existence.

Now I can bear loneliness. For it is not final. And nothing speaks to me as if it were for ever fleeting and transient. We heard indeed that at the beginning of the dying process the dying left the body without being able to make themselves understood by the living they had left behind. But I can still be sure that there is a zone of common ground which I shall one day tread, like them. And just as I die my death ahead of time, as if it were reality today, so I also experience ahead this common ground, so that it is already present now, today. My loneliness is broken because these experiences strengthen my belief in the continuance of an indestructible core in me and in my fellow men.

We all live with the separations that are imposed on us, because we have to live with them. But everything depends on *the way* we do so. Separation, as I said at the beginning, is a kind of dying. It can make life impossible for us. Then we take refuge in neurosis. It can make us hostile and indifferent, and we can choose evasions, try to forget it in activity and a passion for amusement or employ a stoic philosophy to cover it up.[134] In each case we allow separation to kill us. We can only accept it and learn to live with it if we acquire a new picture of dying and death, which express themselves in separation. After all that we have discussed together, I have gained the conviction that through our dying and our death a

region opens up for us all which does not suffer separations. Anyone who knows that can put up with loneliness.

The Art of Dying

One day I shall have to yield up my body, that wonderful organ
which has served me for so many decades with a precision that no
human workmanship achieves. But this will not happen without
my receiving new potentialities of life. It is true that I talk about
body and soul. But this dichotomy is simply one that exists in our
terminology. I, the person, am a unity. And even if I cannot say
what it means for this body of mine to decay (which is after all only
my body because it is animated by a soul), yet I know that my
death will not be separation but transformation.

What the dying have told us is no more than what faith has
always known. But they can confirm that knowledge. What we
suspected finds support. No-one can have any direct experience of
death itself, we are told on the page that prefaces this book. But if it
looks as we have been shown it looks, in the gateway leading to
death, then we might after all talk about an indirect pre-experience.
If dying leads so pre-eminently towards the music of the spheres
and a brighter light, if dying leads the fearful man or woman into a
wider world, then death will not be silence, night, and
confinement.

In dying, it has been said recently, one is faced with the 'final
decision' for or against salvation. Consequently in that hour even
the spiritually handicapped and undeveloped receive their full consciousness. And this decision, we are told, can only be the balance
or sum total of the many part-decisions which we already made in
life.[135] This belief has primarily the moral balance sheet in view.
Here it seems to me that the idea of retaliation has not been overcome, though Jesus took people beyond this concept when he
promised even the murderer who hung at his side on the gallows,
'Today you will be with me in Paradise' (Luke 23.42). This crimi-
nal's whole final decision consisted of his admission that his life had
been a failure.

To step out, let myself go, give up my will, not to want to decide any more but to let myself be sustained, to accept the past as good, to let myself be called to new existence, to be led into the light— that is probably what dying is and brings, if we sum up the experiences that have been passed on to us. It seems a matter of indifference with what religious vocabulary we interpret it for ourselves. The sum is not so much a decision on our part; it really means that a decision is made about us and that we accept this.

When we absorb into our lives the idea of dying as a reality of this kind, we see ourselves at the same time forced more strongly than before to take seriously the many part-decisions for or against our salvation which life extorts from us. But the keynote of a new art of dealing in life with dying of this kind nevertheless lies elsewhere. Is a person's 'status' really dependent on his decisions? Is he not generally almost helplessly overrun by them and does he not, with the best intentions, continually make the wrong ones? Would not the final account of every life look bleak if the ultimate, radical decision for salvation or its reverse were to be derived from the sum of a person's part-decisions? The accounts given by the dying have rather told me the following: dying brings forth a reality which I am going to be, but which I also always was. This reality cannot apparently be destroyed by anything at all that I do, permit, and suffer in this first reality which is visible to me.

And I am already that other reality which death—the Christian will say: which God in death—is going to show me; I can grasp it already, this moment. It is not cut off from my everyday reality but is concealed within it, in just the same way as, according to the belief of the spiritualists, the adherent of the spirit and the mystic— the spiritual body is concealed in a person's physical body. The light which the dying perceive is already with me. I can perceive it as soon as I let my will go, as is required of me in dying. We have come to see that we are perpetually experiencing dying while we still live. But now, in conclusion, we must see to it that we do not let the kind of dying that denies life be the one that counts for us and walks beside us; what must accompany us is dying as the confirmation of the other reality.

This requirement is directed to us both as individuals and as a society. Our Late Western society will not be able to live unless it

acquires a quite different picture of dying and death. Is it really
worth living even a single day if our lives only aim at making room
for younger lives? Death as the necessity of a nature which is forced
to maintain its finite character cruelly and dreadfully leaves man
neither dignity nor liberty. We are supposed to understand and
justify death in the light of this notion of Darwin's which still
dominates our public life. But perhaps the very reverse is true:
death is necessary so that we may become conscious of the reality
that we are.

If I let the experiences of the dying accompany my everyday life,
I shall remain aware of this reality, the 'eternity' of my existence,
the indestructibility of my person in all assailments, the freedom
which awaits me, the light of my future, which knows neither fear,
dismay, nor want. I shall learn again that I shall be carried through.
I shall accomplish a new art of dying, but now—since dying presents itself in this way as being quite different—I shall be able to
avoid what is negative in the medieval art of dying. I shall not, as
some Trappists once did, live with an empty coffin in my cell,
because I know that the coffin is the utterly wrong symbol for the
reality which I always am.

I shall live closer to death now, but I shall not fly from the world
or hate the body because of that. For death as I surmise it to be does
not deny; it confirms. The life which we are forced to live today
especially, the life of endless demands and planned minutes, the
compulsions for performance, and the helplessness, will acquire
depth through the idea that experiences of the kind we now know
wait for us in dying and that death will receive us in this way. My
consciousness fills an endless space. And it is not going to perish.
Heaven and hell are here. The transition from here to there is not
the description of a medical fact, and laboratory apparatus can
measure my brain currents but not my existence.

This little book cannot dispute the tradition of what Christianity
has said about this subject from earliest times. But the reader who
in future brings his everyday life into line with the experiences
related here—or even his own experiences—will make one correc-
tion. Reality has always been divided up much too rigidly into
individual facets and facts. According to the catechism, hope was to

be directed towards this and that which were to come. Old words, usually of Latin origin, can be used to describe it. Hope was presented to us as some external object of hope. But it ought to dwell within us as the experience of the reality which we are, and to which we shall be continually called.

We have encountered a piece of human reality which shows the person to be indestructible and unconditional. Our 'sickness unto death' can be healed. This is what Kierkegaard called the despair of modern man and his contempt for the inalienable human right to his own unique personal relationship with God, i.e., his existence. For although today no subject is more frequently canvassed than that of the rights of the individual, there is nothing about which we know so little as his true status, the unconditional character of his existence, his 'eternity', his indestructible reality, which is so apparent in dying that we can live that reality.

'For me to die is gain', says the apostle (Phil. 1.21), because in dying I experience life—which means for him and us, Christ. I die in the midst of life, we said; but the fear of dying and the fear of death are past. I do not have to enter into the narrow confines, for our nightmare images of dying have been wiped out. I am not a death instinct and do not have to give myself up to the longing for death, like an addict, in the hope of transcendental experiences. For I cannot be lost in life. I am sought for. I do not plunge into anonymity. My death will not be a separation. In practising the art of dying I am achieving euthanasia, in the true sense, for myself and my fellow men. I am learning here in life to live the eternity which I gain in dying, my reality, my dignity, and my freedom.

That world, Kierkegaard's 'rooms of roses', will be different from this one. We shall be different people and we do not know what we shall be. But we know that it is *we* who will be and that we shall be like him. And we know that this world and the other world are one. So tomorrow can be effective today. And so I have hope and confidence for this life of mine, because we *may*, not *must*, die; and because dying is quite different from what we have always thought.

NOTES

1. Wilhelm Wundt, *Elemente der Völkerpsychologie* (Leipzig, 1913), p. 81; ET *Elements of Folk Psychology* (London, New York, 1916), p. 81.

2. Artur Reiner, *Ich sehe keinen Ausweg mehr, Suizid und Suizidverhütung–Konsequenzen für die Seelsorge* (Munich, 1974).

3. Arthur Schopenhauer, *Die Welt als Wille und Vorstellung* (Halle, 1831), vol. 11, p. 512; ET *The World as Will and Idea* (London, 1883) and *The World as Will and Representation* (Indian Hills, Colorado, 1958); Franz Rosenzweig, *Stern der Erlösung* (Heidelberg, 1921), vol. iii, p. 18.

4. Friedrich Schauer, *Was ist es um die Hölle?* (Stuttgart, 1956), p. 23. On the problem, Thomas and Gertrude Sartory, *Nach dem Tod–die Hölle?* (Munich, 1968).

5. Eberhard Bethge, *Dietrich Bonhoeffer, Eine Biographie* (Munich, 1967), p. 1083; ET *Dietrich Bonhoeffer* (London, New York, 1975), pp. 830–1.

6. Werner Fuchs, *Todesbilder in der modernen Gesellschaft* (Frankfurt, 1973), p. 204.

7. Arnold Toynbee in A. Toynbee *et al.*, *Man's Concern with Death* (London, 1968).

8. Rainer Maria Rilke, *Sämtliche Werke*, vol. 1 (Frankfurt, 1955), p. 477. (This is the final poem in *Buch der Bilder*.)

9. Alexander Dorozynski, *The Man They Wouldn't Let Die* (London, 1965).

10. Willy Kramp, *Der letzte Feind* (Munich, 1970), p. 7.

11. 'A basic psychological orientation ... ' in *Psychiatric Quarterly* (New York), April 1961, pp. 1ff.

12. Taken from the report of the Bundeskongress des Deutschen Evangelischen Verbands für Altenpflege, May 1975, Berlin, in *Sonntagsblatt der Evang.-Lutherischen Kirche in Bayern*, 5 May 1975, p. 20.

13. Hans Martensen-Larsen, *An der Pforte des Todes* (Hamburg, 1955), p. 73.

14. J. W. von Goethe, *Faust* 1 (1808). Scene: Night, street in front of Gretchen's

door. Opinions of contemporary writers and poets on the problem of death are impressively collected in G. Debus and Arnim Juhre, *Tod in der Gesellschaft*, Almanach 5 für Literatur und Theologie (Wuppertal, 1971).

15. Rainer Maria Rilke, *Die Aufzeichnungen des Malte Laurids Brigge* (Leipzig, 1926), pp. 14ff.

16. See Martensen-Larsen, n.13, p. 75.

17. Teilhard de Chardin, *Le Milieu divin* (Paris, 1957), p. 19; ET *Le Milieu divin: An essay on the interior life* (London, 1960), pp. 69–70.

18. *Letter to Laertes*, X.

19. Ivan Illich's theory at the symposium 'Grenzen der Medizin' (The Limitations of Medicine), Davos, March 1974, in *Brennpunkte* 3/75, Gottlieb-Duttweiler-Institut, Rüschlikon-Zürich.

20. Emil Mattiesen, *Das persönliche Überleben des Todes* (Berlin, 1936), vol. ii, p. 312.

21. *Revue Spirite* (Paris, 1927), pp. 110f.

22. J. A. Kanne, *Leben und aus dem Leben merkwürdiger und erweckter Christen der protestantischen Kirche* (Leipzig, 1942), vol. 1, p. 23; Gottfried Arnold, *Unparteiische Kirchen- und Ketzerhistorie* (1670), 10th Hist., p. 184.

23. Communicated by Dr Werner Duvernoy, Uppsala.

24. *Revue Métapsychique* (Paris, 1930), pp. 190f.

25. See p. 35.

26. See p. 42.

27. See p. 48.

28. See Mattiesen (n. 20), p. 322.

29. Taken from the periodical on parapsychology, *Borderland*, 28, vol. iv, pp. 438f.

30. *Proceedings of the Society for Psychical Research* (London), viii, pp. 180ff. (much shortened).

31. C. L. Tweedale, *Man's Survival After Death or the Other Side of Life*, 3rd edn (London, 1925), pp. 88f.

32. Report by Elisabeth Blakeley in R. Crookall, *Study and Practice of Astral Projection*, case 1 (London, 1961); first published in *Prediction*, March 1953.

33. Ernst Benz, *Die Vision, Erfahrungsformen und Bilderwelt* (Stuttgart, 1969), pp. 267f.

34. See n. 30; pp. 194f. The reader will find many reports of a similar kind in Martensen-Larsen (see n.13); many also have a bearing on the subject treated in chapter 3 of the present book. See also Mattiesen (see n.20); Georges Barbarin, *Le Livre de la mort douce* (Paris, 1937); Enno Nielsen, *Das Unerkannte auf seinem Weg durch die Jahrtausende* (Ebenhausen, 1922) and *Das große Geheimnis* (Ebenhausen, 1923); Hinrich Ohlhaver, *Die Toten leben, eigene Erlebnisse*, 3 vol. (Hamburg, 1921); F. Splittgerber, *Aus dem inneren Leben von Schlaf und Tod*, 2 vol. (Stuttgart, 1884); Carl Vogl, *Unsterblichkeit, vom geheimen Leben der Seele* (Dachau, 1917); Wladimir Lindenberg, *Über die Schwelle, Gedanken über die letzten Dinge* (Munich, 1973); Julius Bahle, *Keine Angst vor dem Sterben* (Hemmenhofen, 1963); Eckart Wiesenhütter, *Blick nach drüben, Selbsterfahrungen im Sterben* (Hamburg, 1974); Joy Snell, *The Ministry of Angels, Here and Beyond* (London, 1950); Hans Theodor Brik, *Und nach dem Tode? Das Rätsel der menschlichen Seele* (Linz, 1972); Wilhelm Otto

Roesenmüller, *Um die Todesstunde ... Blicke in eine andere Welt* (Nuremberg, 1972). Mattiesen has a full bibliography of literature on the subject down to 1935, covering especially French and English writings. France and the English-speaking countries have always shown a particularly open mind about these phenomena.

35. C. G. Jung, *Gesammelte Werke*, vol. xvi (Zürich, 1958), pp. 277f.

36. See Mattiesen (n.20), p. 324, quoting S. J. Muldoon and H. Carrington, *The Projection of the Astral Body* (London, 1929), pp. 188–9.

37. Communicated by the architect Stevan von Jankovich, Zürich-Lugano. This valuable and detailed account can only be given in shortened form and split up into different sections. For its continuation see pp. 59f., 70f., 75, 106f.

38. According to Tantra teaching, the whole universe is flooded by energy deriving from the source of being. It manifests itself in threefold wise: as static equilibrium, spiritual power, and as the harmonious association of these opposites. The macrocosm of the universe has its precise counterpart in the microcosm of man, whose soul is fettered by a bond to created forms, until it can free itself through conformity to the macrocosm and can unite with God. Men and women have three bodies, the physical or gross body, the causal body, and the subtle body. Mattiesen (n.20, pp. 261ff.) tells us about the 'trans-manifestations' and the 'metaorganism' of parapsychological experience. 'Everyone possesses a body of "light-producing aether" enclosed in his physical body.' Numerous testimonies for the experience of the 'silver cord' are cited here too. The silver cord is said to unite the two bodies during the exit of the self. On spiritualism, see pp. 114–19.

39. Communicated by Prof. Paul Anton Keller, Graz. See also his books *Im Schattenreich* (Gütersloh, 1948) and *Der Mann im Moor* (Graz, 1956).

40. Ibid., continuation of the account.

41. See n. 32; continuation.

42. Continuation of account on pp. 38f.

43. William Camden (1551–1623); but see also Börries von Münchhausen, *Das Balladenbuch* (Stuttgart, 1924), p. 184.

44. See n.13.

45. Hias Rebitsch, 'Gedanken und Visionen bei einem Absturz' in *Der Bergsteiger* (official organ of the Austrian Alpine Association; Munich, 1970).

46. Arthur Jores, 'Der Tod in psychologischer Sicht' in A. Sborowitz, *Der leidende Mensch* (Darmstadt, 1960), p. 419.

47. See n.34, pp. 55f.

48. Ibid, p. 56.

49. Report by a patient from the hospital for infectious diseases, Östersund, Sweden; communicated by Dr Werner Duvernoy, Uppsala (shortened).

50. See n.37.

51. Leo N. Tolstoy, tr. Aylmer Maude, *The Death of Ivan Illych* (London, 1960).

52. *The Tibetan Book of the Dead*, tr. W. Y. Evans-Wentz (London, New York, 1957), pp. 90–6.

53. Mrs Else van Gelder, Velp, Netherlands, letter to the author.

54. Victor D. Solow, 'I died at 10.52' in *Reader's Digest*, February 1975, pp. 103ff.

55. See n. 32, continuation.

56. See Bahle, (see n.34), pp. 74f.

57. See p. 50.
58. See n.39.
59. Prof. Albert Heim in 'Notizen über den Tod durch Alpabsturz', *Jahrbuch des Schweizer Alpklubs*, 27th year, 1891/2.
60. See Bahle (see n.34), pp. 76f.
61. See n.53.
62. See Wiesenhütter (see n.34), pp. 15f.
63. See pp. 47f.
64. See pp. 59f.
65. See n.37.
66. See Martensen-Larsen (see n.13), pp. 89f.
67. Patient's report, communicated by Dr Werner Duvernoy, Uppsala.
68. See Barbarin (see n.34), p. 67.
69. Report of Mr Hartley, rescued from the Ohio, in Barbarin (see n.34), p. 91, following *Revue scientifique* (1894), p. 700.
70. Balthasar Staehelin, *Haben und Sein* (Zürich, 1969), p. 43: 'It is the very certainty of death that gives a person the possibility of recovery—recovery as a person, not merely biological recovery in the sense of a properly functioning organism.'
71. See n.37, continuation of the text on pp. 59f.
72. See n.54.
73. See n.34.
74. See Martensen-Larsen (see n.13), pp. 88f.
75. See Barbarin, (see n.34), pp. 156f.
76. See pp. 51f.
77. See pp. 34, 40f.
78. See S. Radhakrishnan, *The Bhagavadgita* (1948).
79. *Tibetan Book of the Dead* (see n.52), pp. 89f., n.3.
80. Jakob Böhme, *Vom übersinnlichen Leben, Schriften*, vol. 5 (Leipzig, 1923).
81. See Bahle, (see n.34), pp. 20ff.
82. See Martensen-Larsen (see n.13), pp. 104f.
83. See Wiesenhütter (see n.34), pp. 49f.
84. Detailed discussion in Florin Laubenthal, *Hirn und Seele–Ärztliches zum Leib-Seele-Problem* (Salzburg, 1953); Franz Andreas Völgyese, *Die Seele ist alles–Von der Dämonologie zur Heilhypnose,* 2nd edn (Zürich, 1967).
85. G. Topf, 'Rauschdrogen, Zwischen Himmel und Hölle' from *Medizinstudent* 10, 2/1975 (Erlangen, 1975), pp. 23ff.
86. Achim Seidl, 'Im seelischen Untergrund, Einblick in unsere Psyche', in *Psychoanalyse und Gesellschaft* (Munich, 1972), pp. 37f.
87. See n.34.
88. After G. N. M. Tyrrel, *Mensch und Welt in der Parapsychologie* (Hamburg, 1961), report of 27 February 1927.
89. See pp. 57f., n.49.
90. See n.32.
91. See p. 68.
92. See n.59.
93. Continuation of Solow account, see n.54.

94. See n.9.

95. See p. 37.

96. Conclusion of Sir Auckland Geddee's report, see pp. 83f.

97. Continuation of pp. 48ff., see n.39.

98. Continuation of pp. 66f., see n.56.

99. Report from the intensive care unit, Uppsala Hospital, communicated by Dr Werner Duvernoy.

100. See Wiesenhütter (see n.34), pp. 69f.

101. See p. 41.

102. See pp. 71f.

103. See Martensen-Larsen (see n.13), p. 90.

104. See Wiesenhütter (see n.34), p. 77.

105. See Solow account (see n.54).

106. 'Herrn Abraham v. Franckenbergs auf Ludwigsdorf, Lebensbeschreibung Jakob Böhmes' in *Schriften Jakob Böhmes* (Leipzig, 1923), p. 39.

107. Dienstagsredaktion des Süddeutschen Rundfunks, broadcast by the author on 19 November 1974.

108. Barbarin (see n.34), p. 40, goes on: 'Death is a harmonious termination as long as it remains in the sphere of instinct.' According to the insights we have gained in the present book, the sentence ought to run: dying is free of pain, even when the person presses beyond the sphere of instinct and achieves 'super-consciousness'.

109. Impressive report in Bahle (see n.34), pp. 48ff., 85f.

110. See p. 74.

111. See pp. 53, 59, 66f., 72.

112. See p. 41.

113. Dr Werner Duvernoy in a studio discussion with the author, NDR television on 1 November 1974.

114. See p. 75.

115. See n.37; continuation of the text on p. 75.

116. 'Gedanken über Tod und Unsterblichkeit', *Jugendschriften* (Stuttgart, 1962), p. 90.

117. *Genèse d'une pensée* (Paris, 1961).

118. Teilhard de Chardin in Adolf Haas, *Teilhard de Chardin-Lexikon* (Freiburg, 1971), vol. ii, p. 338.

119. Arthur Schopenhauer, *Versuch über Geistersehen und was damit zusamnenhängt, Parerga und Paralipommena* (Halle, n.d.), p. 255.

120. London, 1950.

121. Gerhard Bergmann makes the attempt in ... *und es gibt doch ein Jenseits–Auf den Spuren des Übersinnlichen* (Gladbeck, 1971).

122. Paracelsus Theophrastus von Hohenheim, selection by Charles Waldemar (Munich, 1958), p. 576.

123. Heinrich Zimmer, *Philosophie und Religion Indiens* (Zürich, 1971), p. 172.

124. Emmanuel Swedenborg, 'Das Leben nach dem Tode' in *Vision und Ekstase* (Munich, 1959), p. 22.

125. See Barbarin (see n.34), p. 70.

126. Ibid, p. 33.

127. See n.19.

128. New York, London, 1969.

129. See here Josef Meyer-Scheu, 'Bedingungen einer Sterbenshilfe im Krankenhaus' in Wilhelm Bitter, *Alter und Tod–annehmen oder verdrängen? Ein Tagungsbericht* (Stuttgart, 1974), pp. 59ff.

130. Margaretta K. Bowers *et al.*, *Wie können wir Sterbenden beistehen* (Munich, Mainz, 1973), p. 102. The book contains a comprehensive bibliography on the present-day problem.

131. See p. 23.

132. Teilhard de Chardin, *Le Milieu divin*, pp. 68–9. See n.17.

133. Hugo von Hofmannsthal, *Der Tor und der Tod*; ET *Death and the Fool*, tr. Michael Hamburger in Hugo von Hoffmansthal, *Poems and Verse Plays* (London, 1961).

134. Igor A. Caruso, *Der Tod der Liebenden* (Bern, 1968), p. 27.

135. Karl Rahner, 'Ideas for a Theology of Death' in *Theological Investigations*, 13 (London 1975), pp. 169ff.

www.ingramcontent.com/pod-product-compliance
Lightning Source LLC
Chambersburg PA
CBHW030836090426
42737CB00009B/1000